Tea with Jane Austen

Tea with Jane Austen

KIM WILSON

JONES
BOOKS
Madison, Wisconsin

Jones Books
309 N. Hillside Terrace
Madison, Wisconsin 53705-3328
www.jonesbooks.com

First edition, fourth printing

Library of Congress Cataloging-in-Publication Data

Wilson, Kim, 1959-
    Tea with Jane Austen / Kim Wilson.—1st ed.
        p. cm.
    Includes bibliographical references and index.
    ISBN 0-9721217-9-X (alk. paper)
    1. Austen, Jane, 1775-1817. 2. Austen, Jane, 1775-1817—Knowledge—Manners
and customs. 3. Novelists, English—19th century—Biography. 4. Drinking customs
in literature. 5. Drinking customs—England. 6. Afternoon teas—England. 7. Tea
in literature. 8. Tea—England. I. Title.
    PR4036.W56 2004
    823'.7—dc22

                                                    2004015677

Printed in the U.S.A.

To my parents

Table of Contents

"That Best of All Travelling Liquors": Tea Away from Home
Rakes and Courtesans in the Garden • Tea al Fresco • Tea on the Road • Tea for the Stranded • In Mrs. La Tournelle's Parlor • Tea and Grog • Officers and Gentlemen • Emma's Box Hill Picnic and Captain Wentworth's Mess

"The Tea!—The Tea!—The Wholesome Tea!": Tea and Health
Tempest in a Teapot • The Apothecary's Arsenal • Herbs and Dandelions • Tea and the Delicate Constitution • Tea for Oppressed Heroines • Spiritual Refreshment and Inspiration • Tea with That Little Something Extra • Proper Nourishment for the Sick

"You Must Drink Tea with Us Tonight": Tea in the Evening
At the End of the Day • Waiting for Tea • A Quiet Family Evening • Pleasant Little Parties • An Elegant Entertainment • "Every thing so good!" • A Splendid Supper • Dishes for a Grand Entertainment

"A Good Dish of Tea": Making the Perfect Cup

Bibliography

Index

Foreword

One of the delightful but trivial details visitors to Jane Austen's House in the village of Chawton in Hampshire discover is that the Austens' tea, and coffee if they had any, was kept under lock and key in the cupboard on the left of the fireplace in their "dining parlour"; the "dining room" as we would call it today.

Whilst to us tea is an everyday commodity in our larder with a wide variety to choose from on the shop shelf, and added without much thought to the shopping list when re-supply is needed, it was regarded as something rather more special in Jane Austen's time. As Kim Wilson tells us, not only was it relatively expensive, but to be able to offer it to visitors implied some degree of social status. A whole industry had developed to supply the ingredient for the pleasant beverage, tea pots from which to serve, and the tea sets to drink from.

It is easy to pass over what may appear to be minor or peripheral description to the major story in Jane Austen's novels, but as this book shows, there is frequent reference to this simple demonstration of hospitality that underpinned the expected social custom of the time.

There are also some wickedly tempting recipes included by the author.

For those who love to re-discover "how it was done then," this is a book to amuse and enjoy which I commend to the reader.

—Tom Carpenter (Trustee at Jane Austen's House, Chawton, England) 2004

Acknowledgments

Thanks are due first to my many friends in the Jane Austen Society of North America for their encouragement and advice, and especially to my dear friend Joan Philosophos, who urged me to write about Jane Austen. I am also grateful to those who have assisted me in the preparation of the book: Tom Carpenter of Jane Austen's House in Chawton; Josiah Wedgwood & Sons Ltd.; Twinings; Candice Hern; my insightful editors, Chris Roerden and Carrie Bebris; and my publisher, Joan Strasbaugh. Most importantly, I must thank my husband and children for their endless patience and loving support.

I am particularly grateful to the following authors: T.A.B. Corley for the description of Jane Austen's boarding school in *Women's Writing*; Mark Girouard for his discussion of landscaping fashions in *Life in the English Country House*; Maggie Lane for her chapter on "Mealtimes, Menus, Manners" in *Jane Austen and Food*; Deirdre Le Faye for her discussion of the society of Jane Austen's time in *Jane Austen: The World of Her Novels*; Jane Pettigrew for her discussion of tea history and social customs in *A Social History of Tea*; James Norwood Pratt for his comprehensive guide to the world of tea, the *New Tea Lover's Treasury*; Brian Southam for his chapter on "Naval Education and the Sailor Brothers" in *Jane Austen and the Navy*; and Amanda Vickery for her discussion of tea and shopping in *The Gentleman's Daughter*.

Notes on the Text

Most original spellings, capitalizations, and punctuations of Jane Austen and her contemporaries appear unchanged in this book. Some abbreviations have been expanded for clarity.

The confectioner's shop dialogue in "Cents & Sensibility" is drawn from Maria Edgeworth's story "Angelina," in *Moral Tales for Young People* (1805).

$\mathscr{I}$ntroduction

Jane Austen loved tea. She mentions tea so often in her novels and in her letters that I began to suspect that she was a true tea enthusiast. Sure enough, there, in one of her letters to her sister, are the telltale signs. "Let me know when you begin the new Tea," she writes eagerly. "I am still a Cat if I see a Mouse." Proof enough: Jane was an avid tea lover, ready to pounce on a really good cup of tea.

At the center of almost every social situation in her novels one finds— tea. In *Emma*, does Miss Bates drink coffee? Of course not: "No coffee, I thank you, for me—never take coffee.—A little tea if you please." In *Sense and Sensibility*, what is everyone drinking when Elinor notices Edward's mysterious ring set with a lock of hair? Tea, of course. And in *Pride and Prejudice*, what is one of the supreme honors Mr. Collins can envision Lady Catherine bestowing on Elizabeth Bennet and her friends? Why, drinking tea with her, naturally.

This book examines the role tea played in everyday life for Jane Austen (1775–1817) and her characters. Illustrated with extracts from her novels, her letters, and the writings of her contemporaries, each chapter looks at tea in a different context, from taking tea at various times of day to its function in particular aspects of their lives. I also include some recipes of the time, along with adaptations for the modern cook, for tasty fare that was served with tea.

Tea wasn't always a part of British life. When Queen Elizabeth I ruled England in the 1500s, the British were aware of China only as a distant, almost mythical land; they had certainly never heard of tea. Queen Elizabeth drank good English ale with her meals and never dreamed she was missing anything. However, the two hundred years before Jane Austen's birth saw an astonishing array of changes in England and the rest of Europe. Improvements in navigation and shipbuilding brought the most distant parts of the world within reach, and new, exotic goods and foods flowed in, changing the daily lives of Europeans forever.

In Great Britain and on the continent, the new foods and beverages were eagerly embraced. Tea from China, chocolate from the New World, and coffee from Arabia captured the imaginations and the taste buds of Europeans, quickly becoming all the rage with the upper classes. Coffee houses, which sold tea and hot chocolate as well as coffee, sprang up by the hundreds in London. Coffee was the fashion for some decades, but by 1700 the British elites were beginning to prefer tea. Charles II's wife, Catherine of Braganza, was England's first tea-drinking queen, and it is often said that she helped to popularize it with the aristocracy.

The new, fashionable, and very expensive beverage naturally required new, fashionable, and very expensive equipment to properly serve it. Delicate porcelain cups, saucers, and teapots were imported by the thousands from China. Woodworkers carved elegant tea tables and graceful tea stands of mahogany imported from far-flung British possessions. Silversmiths handcrafted tea sets that we still consider works of art today. Ladies competed with each other to show off their expensive tea and costly tea things at stylish tea parties. In London and other cities, lavish tea gardens were laid out—places in which those who could afford the price of admission strolled under colored lanterns, listened to music, watched fireworks, and drank tea in private boxes. As the price of tea gradually fell, tea-drinking grew in popularity with the working classes as well. By Jane Austen's time, tea was so firmly embedded in British culture that it was considered practically a necessity of life, a belief still widely held today.

Tea evokes a place and a mood that are essentially British. On a cold, damp day, few things are more welcome than a cheerful cup of hot tea. In his poem "The Task: The Winter Evening," one of Jane Austen's favorite poets, William Cowper, described the cozy feeling of tea in the evening:

———————

Now stir the fire, and close the shutters fast,
Let fall the curtains, wheel the sofa round,
And, while the bubbling and loud hissing urn
Throws up a steamy column, and the cups,
That cheer but not inebriate, wait on each,
So let us welcome peaceful ev'ning in.

———————

Take out your cup and put the kettle on, and we'll join Jane Austen for tea.

"Happy, happy breakfast!"
Tea in the Morning

Happy, happy breakfast! for Henry had been
there, Henry had sat by her and helped her.

— *Northanger Abbey*

Breakfast with the Austens

Jane Austen was in charge of making her family's breakfast every morning, including that most important part of breakfast: the tea. Producing a really good, hot, steaming pot of fragrant tea requires just the right touch, and Jane, a tea lover, was no doubt pleased to make the family's tea exactly as she liked it. She would have made it much the way we make good tea today, with freshly boiling water poured bubbling over high-quality, loose tea in a nice, fat, warmed teapot. Jane probably would have boiled the water in the Austens' large, copper tea kettle right in the dining room, on the black hob grate set into the fireplace.

She may have used a teapot from a special breakfast set (a friend gave Jane's mother a Wedgwood breakfast set in 1811). China breakfast sets usually included a teapot, cups and saucers, a creamer, a sugar basin, and sometimes a matching tray. Such sets were fragile as well as valuable. Jane's nephew wrote in his memoir of her, "Some ladies liked to wash with their own hands their choice china after breakfast or tea," and Jane may well have preferred to wash the china herself rather than entrust it to the maid.

The tea itself (at that time extremely expensive and therefore prone to pilfering by servants), was kept locked away in a dining room cupboard, to which Jane alone had the keys. The Austens may have kept their tea in a china tea canister, or, more probably, in a locked tea caddy, which seems to have been the most common kind of tea container. Tea caddies were often made of fine inlaid woods or decorated in some other attractive fashion. A popular craft for young ladies was to decorate a tea caddy with filigree work:

rolled strips of paper applied in a fanciful pattern. In *Sense and Sensibility*, Lucy Steele, sly flatterer that she is, makes a filigree basket for Lady Middleton's spoiled daughter and no doubt would have eagerly decorated a tea caddy for Lady Middleton had she been asked.

Caddies were generally divided into two sections to hold two different sorts of tea (usually green and black), and often included a crystal bowl for blending the tea. A small brass or silver scoop, called a tea ladle, was used to measure out the tea leaves. In 1808 Jane Austen recorded her mother's purchase of a "silver Tea-Ladle" and "six whole Teaspoons, which makes our sideboard border on the Magnificent."

Jane most likely took sugar in her tea—most English people did in her time—but I don't think she took milk or cream. Writing to her sister, Cassandra,

> At 9 o'clock she made breakfast—*that* was *her* part of the household work—The tea and sugar stores were under *her* charge.
>
> — *My Aunt Jane Austen*,
>   by Caroline Austen

about a young lady of their acquaintance, she said, "There are two Traits in her Character which are pleasing; namely, she admires [the novel] Camilla, & drinks no cream in her Tea."

The Austens kept their sugar locked up because it, too, was expensive. It was sold in many grades, from the highly refined, pure white sugar that only the well-off could afford, down to the darkest of brown sugars used by the poor. Granulated sugar had been only recently invented and was not yet widely available. Sugar was molded into large, cone-shaped loaves weighing several pounds each that had to be broken up or grated before the sugar could be used. Sugar cubes would not be invented until 1843—if people wanted sugar for tea, they had to first break it into irregular lumps with

The breakfasts are generally very frugal, consisting commonly of tea, and muffins or hot rolls, with good butter. Coffee is less frequently used; and it is seldom good. I could rarely get it strong or clear, and in this only does there seem to be any proof that the English do not understand cooking.

— Letters from England, by Joshua White, 1810

special tools called "sugar nippers," from which practice comes the traditional question "One lump or two?"

The breakfast Jane made for her family was a light, elegant meal consisting of toast, or perhaps muffins or rolls, in addition to the tea. The Austens had a cook, who would have done the actual baking. She probably sliced the bread in the kitchen and brought it to the table in a toast rack, ready for Jane to toast. To make the toast, Jane would have used a long-handled toasting fork or a hearth toaster (a metal rack designed to hold the bread in place) to toast the bread over the open fire—a tricky business. In Jane Austen's unfinished novel *Sanditon*, fussy Arthur Parker shows Charlotte Heywood his mastery of the skill: "I hope you will eat some of this Toast," said he. "I reckon myself a very good Toaster; I never burn my Toasts—I never put them too near the Fire at first—& yet, you see, there is not a Corner but what is well browned."

With the toast went good country butter, and sometimes raspberry jam made in the Austen household or honey from Cassandra's beehives. Jane and Cassandra's mother, who suffered from digestive disorders and "bilious complaints," preferred to eat dry toast for breakfast, but hypochondriac Arthur Parker has the opposite fear—that dry toast will "hurt the coats of the stomach." Arthur, a stout young man, amuses Charlotte when he assures her that the best way to protect his stomach from toast that "irritates and acts like a nutmeg grater" is to eat as much butter as possible on his toast, much to his sisters' disapproval: "Charlotte c[oul]d hardly contain herself as she saw him watching his sisters while he scrupulously scraped off almost as much butter as he put on, & then seizing an odd moment for adding a great dab just before it went into his Mouth."

When the Austens lived in the country, at Steventon and later at Chawton, good butter would have been readily available, but when they lived in the cities of Bath and Southampton, quality milk and butter would have been harder to procure. Fresh dairy products were difficult to import from the countryside, especially in warm weather. To help solve this problem, cows were often kept in cities to provide for the city dwellers. Yet the diet of city cows was so poor that they generally produced unappetizing, watery milk and inferior butter. In *Mansfield Park*, Fanny Price, banished to the city of Portsmouth, must drink her tea with unappealing milk that is "a mixture of motes floating in thin blue." Jane once wrote to Cassandra complaining about Bath butter: "My breakfast supplied only two ideas, that the rolls were good, & the butter bad."

Breakfast with Mr. Darcy

Though breakfast in British households might mean variations on the theme of tea and toast, the meal could sometimes be a luxurious affair. At the grander houses, such as Mr. Darcy's Pemberley in *Pride and Prejudice*, boiling water for tea in a simple copper kettle on the hearth would have been unthinkable. Instead, large, often lavishly decorated silver tea urns were used. Tea urns, despite

their name, held not tea but boiling water. The water was usually kept boiling by means of an insert that contained a red-hot iron bar that had been heated in the kitchen fire. A servant would carry in the steaming tea urn and place it at the end of the table next to the lady of the house, who would make the tea herself in a fine china or silver teapot.

Special china sets made just for breakfast, such as the Austens had, were very popular. Fanny Dashwood complains bitterly in *Sense and Sensibility* that the breakfast china her mother-in-law takes with her when she moves is "twice as handsome as what belongs to this house." In *Northanger Abbey*, Catherine Morland is impressed by the abbey's lavish breakfast and "the elegance of the breakfast set."

The beverages served in such handsome breakfast china invariably included tea (as at the Austen house), but some people, such as Jane's rich brother, Edward, preferred coffee, and others, such as *Northanger Abbey*'s General Tilney, drank hot chocolate (called simply

"Miss Fanny Brooke and myself made tea and coffee; her ladyship presiding at the chocolate tray. A more elegant private breakfast was never given to any company. The urns, trays, waiters, and canisters were all of silver, engraved with Sir Charles's arms; the china was beautiful; in short, the whole equipage was handsome beyond any one I ever saw."

— Charlotte Lawson in *Vicissitudes in Genteel Life* (Anonymous), 1794 "chocolate" at that time). Coffee and chocolate had both been introduced in Great Britain at roughly the same time as tea, but they never became as popular.

Breakfast was not a formal meal. People chatted, or read letters or newspapers. When Catherine Morland receives a disturbing letter at the abbey during breakfast, she is grateful that the intimidating General Tilney, "between his cocoa and his newspaper, had luckily no leisure for noticing her."

Even in great houses, the food served at breakfast was chiefly some variation of bread and butter. Cakes, bread, muffins, toast, and rolls are all mentioned in descriptions of breakfasts of Jane Austen's time. However, more substantial fare was sometimes offered. In *Mansfield Park*, Fanny Price, after bidding goodbye to her brother and Henry Crawford, returns to the breakfast parlor to "cold pork bones and mustard in William's plate" and "broken egg-shells in Mr. Crawford's." Clearly, Henry Crawford had been eating boiled eggs, and William probably had enjoyed some sort of pork chop with his mustard. Cautious Mr. Woodhouse in *Emma* would have approved of the latter as long as it was "nicely fried, as ours are fried, without the smallest grease, and not roast[ed] . . . for no stomach can bear roast pork."

Tea and Toast, or Strong Beer and Sturgeon?

The typical "tea and toast" breakfast that Jane Austen enjoyed was a relatively new invention. Traditionally, British breakfasts had consisted of hearty fare that often included beef and ale. By the end of the eighteenth century, however, many people, especially those of the upper classes, considered such breakfasts to be antiquated and

'*Twas better for each British virgin*
When on roast beef, strong beer and sturgeon,
Joyous to breakfast they sat round,
Nor were ashamed to eat a pound.

— "The Tea-Pot and Scrubbing-Brush," an 18th-century poem by
Christopher Smart

rustic. In the early 1700s, Queen Anne first set the mode of drinking tea for her morning meal, preferring the light, refreshing drink to the heavy, alcoholic beverages that were usually taken in the morning. Ladies and gentlemen followed her lead, and tea soon became a necessary part of the truly fashionable breakfast. To accompany the stylish new beverage, the upper classes developed a taste for a more delicate breakfast, gradually abandoning meat and other heavier breakfast foods.

Naturally, a trend that changed ancient customs often met with strong resistance. Though fashionable ladies and gentlemen saw the beef-and-ale breakfast as outmoded, the heartier style of breakfast lingered on in many old-fashioned and working-class households. A vigorous debate about the relative merits of "tea breakfasts" and traditional British breakfasts lasted for decades. One American visitor to England described a gentleman who was particularly cranky about the changes being forced on him:

Our breakfast consisted of what the squire denominated true
old English fare. He indulged in some bitter lamentations over
modern breakfasts of tea and toast, which he censured as
among the causes of modern effeminacy and weak nerves and
the decline of old English heartiness; and, though he admitted
them to his table to suit the palates of his guests, yet there was
a brave display of cold meats, wine, and ale on the sideboard.

— *Sketchbook*, by Washington Irving, 1819

When Catherine Morland sits down to breakfast with Henry Tilney and
his family in *Northanger Abbey*, the meal she eats is a thoroughly modern
English breakfast, with all the necessary accompaniments of tea caddies,
silver spoons, a delicate china breakfast set, and French bread. Though
"never in her life before had she beheld half such variety on a breakfast-
table," it is a modern variety: an assortment of breads, cakes, butter, cream,
and, of course, tea.

Town and Country Style

Breakfast in the Austen household was usually eaten at nine o'clock, but
Jane frequently rose early and accomplished a great deal beforehand. She
often practiced her music on the pianoforte, or wrote letters at her small,
wooden writing desk. Whenever Jane and Cassandra were separated, they
wrote to each other constantly. Jane wrote many of her letters before
breakfast, a fact she often mentioned in the letter itself: "Here I am before
breakfast writing to you, having got up between six and seven."

Many people in Great Britain in Jane Austen's time also began their days
well before breakfast. While farmhands headed to the fields and servants
busied themselves lighting fires and preparing breakfast for their masters, the
gentry engaged in their own tasks. In the country, ladies and gentlemen rose
as early as seven or eight o'clock, but they often did not eat breakfast until

an hour or two later.

A wealthy gentlewoman such as the elegant Lady Middleton in *Sense and Sensibility* would have spent a good share of the time before breakfast in her dressing room. The Austen women could not afford lady's maids, but a wealthy woman would have had an "abigail," as lady's maids were nicknamed, to dress her hair and array her in a morning gown, in which charmingly casual attire she would pass the morning.

She would then turn to the first business of the day, although admittedly the "work" of a wealthy woman was not very demanding. She might stroll through her gardens picking flowers to fill her fashionable china bowls, write letters (as Emma Woodhouse does in *Emma*), or practice her music. In consultation with her housekeeper, she would discuss household duties and approve the menus for the day. Her husband might ride out or take a walk (as John Knightley does with his little boys in *Emma*), issue the day's orders to his head groom, or meet with his steward.

Breakfast followed at nine o'clock, as the precise, demanding General

The morning hours of the Cottage were always later than those of the other house; and on the morrow the difference was so great, that Mary and Anne were not more than beginning breakfast when Charles came in to say that they were just setting off, that he was come for his dogs, that his sisters were following with Captain Wentworth.

— *Persuasion*

Tilney prefers in *Northanger Abbey*, or even ten, as Sir John and Lady Middleton do at Barton Park in *Sense and Sensibility*. In some households, people came down to breakfast when they pleased, but in most it seems to have been common practice to eat breakfast together at the same time. "It has struck ten; I must go to breakfast," wrote Jane to Cassandra from their brother Edward's house. Sometimes a bell sounded a half-hour's warning, followed by a second bell calling the family and guests to gather for breakfast.

City households such as that of Jane's brother Henry and his fashionable wife, Eliza, tended to keep later hours than those of country houses. Dinner and evening engagements fell later in the day, so people stayed up later and consequently rose later. Lydia and the Gardiners "breakfasted at ten as usual" before Lydia's wedding in *Pride and Prejudice*; but the ultra-fashionable ate as late as eleven or twelve o'clock. Before breakfast the activities of the gentry were much the same as in the country, though in the city ladies might go shopping before breakfast to try to beat the crowds. During a visit to London, Jane wrote to Cassandra that she went shopping before breakfast for material for a gown at Grafton House, "where, by going very early, we got immediate attendance & went on very comfortably."

Some fashionable ladies and gentlemen brought town hours with them when they visited their country estates. In *Pride and Prejudice*, Elizabeth Bennet learns just after breakfast at her own home that her sister is ill at Mr. Bingley's manor house, Netherfield Park. Elizabeth walks three miles cross-country, "jumping over stiles and springing over puddles," to reach Netherfield, yet arrives to find Mr. Bingley and his guests at their own—much later—breakfast. "That she should have walked three miles so early in the day, in such dirty weather, and by herself, was almost incredible to Mrs. Hurst and Miss Bingley; . . . Mr. Darcy said very little, and Mr. Hurst nothing at all. . . . The latter was thinking only of his breakfast."

A Grand Breakfast with the Austens at Stoneleigh Abbey

Breakfast at the Austen home itself consisted mostly of tea and toast, but Jane had many opportunities to experience the grander sort of breakfast commonly served at the great houses. She often visited her brother Edward and his family at Godmersham, the estate he acquired when some childless cousins adopted him as their heir. And when Mrs. Austen's cousin inherited a large manor house in Warwickshire, he invited her, Cassandra, and Jane to visit. Mrs. Austen wrote to her daughter-in-law in raptures over the beauty and size of the house—"26 Bed Chambers in the new part of the house, & a great many (some very good ones) in the Old"—and the vast surrounding estate. Like Mrs. Jennings in *Sense and Sensibility*, she seemed particularly impressed by the food.

STONELEIGH ABBEY,
August 13, 1806.

MY DEAR MARY, . . . here we all found ourselves on Tuesday (that is yesterday sennight) Eating Fish, venison & all manner of good things, at a late hour, in a Noble large Parlour hung round with family Pictures—every thing is very Grand & very fine & very Large—The House is larger than I could have supposed. . . . I expected to find everything about the place very fine & all that, but I had no idea of its being so beautiful . . . at nine in the morning we meet and say our prayers in a handsome Chapel . . . then follows Breakfast, consisting of Chocolate Coffee & Tea—Plumb Cake, Pound Cake, Hot Rolls, Cold Rolls, Bread & Butter, and *dry toast for me*—The House-Steward (a fine large respectable looking Man) orders all these matters . . . . I do not fail to spend some time every day in the Kitchen Garden, where the quantities of small fruits exceed anything you can form an idea of; this large family, with the assistance of a great many Blackbirds & Thrushes cannot prevent its rotting on the Trees—the Garden contains 5 acres and a half—The ponds supply excellent Fish, the Park excellent Venison—There is also great plenty of Pigeons Rabbits and all sort of Poultry—a delightful Dairy, where is made Butter, good Warwickshire Cheese and Cream Ditto.

It's not difficult to recreate the breakfast Jane, Cassandra, and their mother ate at Stoneleigh Abbey. Gather your prettiest china, good tea and coffee (and hot chocolate if you like), and a nice assortment of cakes, rolls, and bread. Don't forget butter of the best quality. An elegant morning gown is optional.

Recipes for Morning

A Pound Cake

Beat a pound of butter in an earthen pan with your hand one way till it be like a fine thick cream. Then have ready twelve eggs; but leave out half the whites; beat them well; then beat them up with the butter, a pound of flour beat in it, a pound of sugar, and a few carraways. Beat all well together with your hand for an hour, or you may beat it with a wooden spoon. Put it all into a buttered pan, and bake it in a quick oven for one hour.

— *The London Art of Cookery*, 1807

The origin of the term "pound cake" lies in the weight of each main ingredient: a pound of flour, a pound of sugar, and a pound of butter. The Stoneleigh Abbey pound cake was no doubt much too rich for Mrs. Austen's poor digestion, but Jane and Cassandra probably enjoyed it very much. A pound cake contains no baking powder, so it must be very well mixed. An electric mixer is easiest; be prepared to mix for a very long time indeed if you choose to use a spoon.

Pound Cake for Jane and Cassandra

1 lb/ 450 g/ 2 cups unsalted butter, at room temperature
6 large eggs plus 6 egg yolks, at room temperature
1 lb/ 450 g/ 4-1/3 cups cake flour
1 lb/ 450 g/ 2 cups white sugar
2 teaspoons pure vanilla extract or 1 teaspoon caraway seeds

Preheat oven to 325°F/ 170°C/ Gas Mark 3. Grease a bundt or tube cake pan.

Beat the butter with an electric mixer at medium speed or by hand until very smooth and creamy. In a separate bowl, beat the eggs and egg yolks together well (about 1 minute). Add the eggs and vanilla extract or caraway seeds to the butter and mix thoroughly. Add the cake flour gradually and mix well. Mix in the sugar. Beat the batter on medium speed until very smooth—about 5 minutes, or at least 200 strokes by hand. Pour the batter into the pan, leveling it off well.

Bake for 1 hour and 20 minutes, or until a bamboo skewer inserted in the deepest part of the cake comes out clean. (Check after 1 hour and every few minutes thereafter to ensure the cake does not become overdone.) Invert the pan on a wire rack and carefully lift it off the cake. Do not allow the cake to cool in the pan, as the crust will be ruined.

Plumb Cake

To a pound and a half of fine flour, well dried, put the same quantity of butter, three quarters of a pound of currants washed and well picked; stone and slice half a pound of raisins, eighteen ounces of sugar beat and sifted, and fourteen eggs, leaving out half the whites; shred the peel of a large lemon exceedingly fine, three ounces of candied orange, the same of lemon, a tea-spoonful of beaten mace, half a nutmeg grated, a tea-cupful of brandy, or white wine, and four spoonfuls of orange-flower. First work the butter with your hand to a cream, then beat your sugar well in, whisk your eggs for half an hour, then mix them with your sugar and butter, and put in your flour and spices. The whole will take an hour and a half beating. When your oven be ready, mix in lightly your brandy, fruit, and sweetmeats, then put it into your hoop, and bake it two hours and a half.

— *The London Art of Cookery*, 1807

Plum cake is essentially a fruitcake, but not the unpleasant dried lump we associate with modern fruitcake. This tasty, moist cake would have been a rich addition to breakfast. The recipe below is for a manageable size, and, thanks to the modern electric mixer, won't require beating for an hour and a half. The success of this cake depends on the quality of the ingredients. Try to find good dried or candied fruit, avoiding at all costs the nasty dyed rubbery bits some stores try to pass off as candied fruit.

Plum Cake for an Elegant Breakfast

12 oz/ 350 g/ 1-1/2 cups unsalted butter, at room temperature

9 oz/ 255 g/ 1-1/3 cups white sugar

4 eggs plus 3 egg yolks, at room temperature

12 oz/ 350 g/ 3 cups cake flour

1/2 teaspoon ground mace

1/4 nutmeg, grated (or 1/2 teaspoon ground nutmeg)

1/2 teaspoon lemon extract or finely grated zest of one-half of a large lemon

1/2 teaspoon orange extract or finely grated zest of one-half of an orange

6 oz/ 175 g/ 1 cup dried currants (substitute raisins or dried cranberries if desired)

4 oz/ 110 g/ 3/4 cup raisins

3 oz/ 85 g/ 1/2 cup mixed, chopped dried or candied fruits

4 fl oz/ 110 ml/ 1/2 cup brandy or white wine (apple or white grape juice may be substituted)

Preheat oven to 325°F/ 170°C/ Gas Mark 3. Grease and flour a 10-inch (25-cm) springform pan.

Beat the butter with an electric mixer at medium speed or by hand until very smooth and creamy. Mix in the sugar and beat well. Beat the eggs in a separate bowl for 5 minutes on medium speed, or until light and frothy. Mix eggs into the butter/sugar mixture and beat well (add the lemon and orange extract at this point if used). Add the flour and spices to the butter mixture gradually, stirring well. Beat 8 minutes on medium-high speed, scraping the sides of the bowl now and then. Lightly fold in the lemon and orange zest, fruit, and brandy. Pour into the pan and bake for 1 hour 15 minutes, or until a bamboo skewer inserted in the deepest part of the cake comes out clean. (Check after 1 hour and every few minutes thereafter to ensure the cake does not become overdone.) To avoid dryness, do not overbake. Remove the sides of the pan and let the cake cool on a wire rack.

Hot Bath Cakes

Take a pound of butter, and rub it into an equal weight of flour, with a spoonful of good barm. Warm some cream, and make it into a light paste. Set it to the fire to rise, and when you make them up, take four ounces of carraway comfits, work part of them in, and strew the rest on the top. Make them into a round cake, the size of a French roll. Bake them on sheet tins, and they will eat well hot for breakfast, or at tea in the afternoon.

— *The London Art of Cookery*, 1807

Caraway comfits are candied caraway seeds, made by dipping the seeds repeatedly into candy-stage sugar syrup. They can sometimes be found in Dutch bakeries, or you may wish to go to the trouble of making your own for an additional touch of authenticity.

Modern Bath Cakes

5 teaspoons (2 packages) active dry yeast
2 oz/ 55 g/ 1/3 cup white sugar
8 fl oz/ 225 ml/ 1 cup warm whole milk or cream (110°F/ 43°C)
1 lb/ 450 g/ 4 cups bread flour
4 oz/ 110 g/ 1/2 cup unsalted butter, softened
2 teaspoons candied or plain caraway seeds (reserve some for sprinkling on top)

Preheat oven to 375° F/ 190° C/ Gas Mark 5

In a small bowl, combine the yeast, sugar, and warm milk. Let stand until
frothy, about 10 minutes. Work the butter into the flour with your fingers
until the mixture forms fine crumbs. Add the yeast mixture to the flour
mixture and work up with your hands to a smooth, elastic dough. Knead the
dough for three or four minutes. Depending on the humidity and your flour,
you may need more or less flour. If the dough is too dry, wet your hands with
a little milk and work it into the dough as you knead. Add the caraway seeds
and knead to distribute the seeds. Place the dough in a large bowl covered
with plastic wrap and let rise in a warm place until doubled in volume, about
1 1/2 to 2 hours.

Lightly grease a baking sheet. Punch down the dough and divide into
small rolls. Place the rolls on the baking sheet and sprinkle with the reserved
caraway seeds. Cover with a lightly greased sheet of plastic wrap (greased
side down). Let rise again in a warm place until doubled in volume, about 15
minutes. Bake 15 to 20 minutes or until golden brown. Makes 20–24 rolls.

Cents & Sensibility
Tea and Shopping

———◆———

I am sorry to tell you that I am getting very
extravagant & spending all my Money; & what is worse for
you, I have been spending yours too.

— Letter from Jane Austen to her sister, Cassandra, 18 April 1811

"A bustling hour or two shopping"

When Jane Austen wanted to shop for tea (or for anything else, for that matter), she had three basic choices: buy from the pedlar who came to her door, walk to the nearest village and take her chances with whatever goods the local shops chose to carry, or wait until she had an opportunity to travel to a larger town or city.

From a pedlar, sometimes known as a Scotchman (whether or not he was Scottish), she could choose from a convenient, if limited, assortment of trinkets and useful things: "The Overton Scotchman has been kind enough to rid me of some of my money, in exchange for six shifts and four pair of stockings," Jane wrote to her sister, Cassandra. "The Irish [linen] is not so fine as I should like it; but as I gave as much money for it as I intended, I have no reason to complain."

The shops in countryside villages and small towns carried a greater variety of goods. Jane often walked to Alton, near her Chawton village home, with her sister or with her niece Fanny. "Aunt Jane and I spent a bustling hour or two shopping in Alton," wrote Fanny in her diary. The problem with shops in country villages is that they didn't always have on hand what people wanted. A contemporary of Jane Austen's described the typical village shop as "multifarious as a bazaar; a repository for bread, shoes, tea, cheese, tape, ribands, and bacon; for everything, in short, except the one particular thing which you happen to want at the moment, and will be sure not to find."

Ford's, in *Emma*, while not quite so diverse—there is no mention of food—is an all-purpose clothing shop for the inhabitants of Highbury: "the

> She has nevertheless desired me to ask you to purchase for her two bottles of Steele's Lavender Water when you are in Town, provided you should go to the Shop on your own account.
>
> — Letter from Jane Austen to Cassandra, 14 January 1801

principal woollen-draper, linen-draper, and haberdasher's shop united" and "the very shop that every body attends every day of their lives." At Mrs. Ford's, Frank Churchill and Miss Bates buy gloves, and Harriet Smith, "tempted by every thing and swayed by half a word," dawdles and dithers over muslins and ribbons.

Larger towns, such as Bath, where Jane Austen visited and even lived for a few years, often had delightful shops. "Bath is a charming place, sir;" says the fashion-obsessed Mrs. Allen to Henry Tilney in *Northanger Abbey*, "there are so many good shops here.—We are sadly off in the country." But the very best place to purchase the latest fashions and the widest variety of goods was, of course, London. Jane often stayed at her brother Henry's house in London on her way to visit another brother, Edward, and she generally spent a good share of her usually short stays there shopping.

"This Scene of Dissipation and Vice"

The shops of London were indeed superior, both in variety and in splendor. To entice passersby to stop and spend, shopkeepers offered an almost endless selection of appealing goods attractively displayed in gleaming glass windows. Visiting her brothers gave Jane Austen the welcome chance to buy choice materials and trimmings for elegant dresses and hats for herself and her sister, and to have them made up in the very latest styles by fashionable London dressmakers and milliners.

"I cannot see that London has any great advantage over the country for my part, except the shops and public places."

— Mrs. Bennet in *Pride and Prejudice*

She bought the family china at Wedgwood's showroom and the family tea at Richard Twining's tea warehouse. She saw the sights, visited museums and art exhibitions, and very often attended the theater, afterward critiquing the acting in letters home to Cassandra.

Not that Jane was all that fond of London itself—she referred to it as "the Wen," basically calling it a wart on the nose of England. Smog, fog, dirt, dung, and noise—the London of Jane Austen's time had them all in abundance. London had its moral pitfalls, too. Jane once playfully wrote from London to her sister, "Here I am once more in this Scene of Dissipation & vice, and I begin already to find my Morals corrupted." Still, she could find goods and goodies in London that she could find nowhere else, and a variety of art exhibits, concerts, and plays that was simply unavailable in the countryside.

Miss Austen Shops in Style

Jane Austen's brother Henry lived in a suburb of London, surrounded by fields, but still within easy walking distance of the fashionable West End shops. On her shopping expeditions, Jane walked into town accompanied either by a relative or by her brother's maid, because, of course, a lady never walked about town alone. For shops located too far away for a comfortable walk, her

What a convenient Carriage Henry's is, to his friends in general!

— Letter from Jane Austen to Cassandra, 3 November 1813

brother Henry let her use his barouche, a stylish type of open carriage generally drawn by four horses and used mostly by the wealthy. This was the equivalent of sending her out in a Rolls Royce with a chauffeur. Barouches appear in most of Jane Austen's novels, and it is always the very well-off who own them: Lady Catherine de Bourgh, Henry Crawford (whose barouche causes so much jealousy between Maria and Julia Bertram), the Dowager Viscountess Dalrymple, and, famously, the nouveau riche Sucklings' barouche-landau that Mrs. Elton forever brags about.

The contrast between Jane's own financial circumstances and the picture she presented by riding in such a carriage amused her very much, but she relished the luxurious feeling: "The Driving about, the Carriage been [*sic*] open, was very pleasant.—I liked my solitary elegance very much, & was ready to laugh all the time, at my being where I was.—I could not but feel that I had naturally small right to be parading about London in a Barouche."

Wonderful Wedgwood

The chance to travel to a big city came seldom for most residents of rural areas; whenever anyone traveled to London, friends and family usually seized the opportunity to load them down with commissions and errands. "We were very busy all yesterday;" Jane wrote to Cassandra, "from 1/2 past 11 to 4 in the Streets, working almost entirely for other people, driving from Place to Place . . . & encountering the miseries of Grafton House to get a purple frock for Eleanor Bridges." Her family trusted Jane to buy jewelry and materials for clothing for them, and, more interestingly for our purposes, their china and tea.

In 1811, Jane wrote to Cassandra from London, "Now I beleive I have done all my commissions, except Wedgwood." Presumably Jane found the time to fulfill her errand to the Wedgwood showroom, because after returning home from London she wrote to inform Cassandra, "On Monday I had the pleasure of receiving, unpacking & approving our Wedgwood ware. It all came very safely, & upon the whole is a good match, tho' I think they

Now I beleive I have done all my commissions, except Wedgwood.

— Letter from Jane Austen to Cassandra, 18 April 1811

might have allowed us rather larger leaves, especially in such a Year of fine foliage as this." She doesn't mention what the Austens ordered, nor does Wedgwood have a record, but I like to think that they purchased a new teapot and more teacups as well as dishes, because you can never really have enough, can you?

The Wedgwood and Byerley showroom in York Street, St. James's Square, was a wonder of modern merchandising. There, in a room filled with sparkling glass-fronted display cases and towering Greek columns that echoed the current craze for antiquities, Jane could have pored over catalogues and viewed the very latest fashions for tableware and decorations. The merchandise was laid out on tables, showing the multitude of shapes, sizes, and designs available. Most of the teapots and teacups would look at home on a tea table today. With them could be ordered a host of accessories: slop bowls (for tea dregs), sugar basins, creamers, tea caddies, tea trays—an endless array of possibilities.

The Austens seem to have been remarkably loyal to Wedgwood. We know that not only they but also their wealthy son, Edward Austen Knight, chose Wedgwood for their china sets. Jane accompanied her brother and his daughter to purchase their set: "We then went to Wedgwoods where my Br[other] & Fanny chose a Dinner Set.—I beleive the pattern is a small Lozenge in purple, between Lines of narrow Gold;—& it is to have the Crest." (Part of the Knight set is on display at the Jane Austen House Museum in Chawton.) When the Austens' friend Martha Lloyd bought Mrs. Austen the special gift of a china breakfast set, she, too, bought it from Wedgwood. If the Austens ever bought china from another manufacturer,

Jane doesn't mention it. In *Northanger Abbey*, General Tilney, an unabashed snob, chooses English china; he "thought it right to encourage the manufacture of his country; and for his part . . . the tea was as well flavoured from the clay of Staffordshire, as from that of Dresden or Sêve." He undoubtedly bought Wedgwood.

For the tea to fill her Wedgwood teacups, Jane waited until she could shop for it in London rather than buy it from a small local shop like Ford's or—heaven forbid—from a roving pedlar. To understand why the Austens chose to purchase their tea from one of the best tea warehouses in London rather than buy it locally, one needs to know a few unpleasant details about the tea of their time.

Tea on Horseback

Tea, at first a luxury for the rich, then later almost a necessity of life for the average British citizen, was an irresistible target for taxes. The ruinously heavy taxes, sometimes over one hundred percent, kept legally purchased tea out of the reach of the poor and gave a huge boost to the already wildly popular business of smuggling. In Jane Austen's time, tea in England sold for six shillings or so a pound for the very cheapest sorts, up to twenty shillings a pound or more for the finest (more than double a week's wage for an unskilled worker). In contrast, one could buy tea in Holland for a fraction of the cost.

Smugglers knew a good thing when they saw it, and quickly added tea to their other profitable cargoes of brandy, tobacco, perfume, silks, and lace. If caught, free traders (as they preferred to be called) faced transportation to the colonies or even hanging, yet smuggling was so widespread it could have been counted as one of Great Britain's major industries. In some areas near the coasts, so many men were involved in free trading that it was hard to find workers for the farms. Smuggling gave goods a certain cachet, lifting ordinary merchandise out of the mundane and into the realm of forbidden

Of all the gay fashions that e're came in vogue,
Since Eve in the garden did play us the rogue,
There is none in the fashion I ever did see
As the women for smuggling and drinking the tea.

— the early 19th-century song "The Tea Drinkers"

fruit. Ladies were delighted to show off their contraband silks, laces, and perfumes, and gentlemen bragged about their smuggled French brandy. Richard Twining estimated that at least half the tea drunk in England was smuggled; almost everyone, it seemed—even clergymen—bought smuggled tea. Why, then, did some families choose to buy the more expensive, legally imported tea? The answers are easy: for the taste and quality. To keep sea water out of it on the crossing to England, smuggled tea was packed in large oilskin bags, which gave it an off taste. On landing, the tea was usually repacked in sacks, which were then slung over horses for the trip inland. Add horse sweat to the lingering flavor of oilskin, and you get an idea of why many people preferred the taste of legal tea.

Smouch and Sheep's Dung

The quality of the tea sold in England in Jane Austen's day was variable, to put it mildly. The best legal tea was usually pure (although the Chinese sometimes dyed green tea for export), and was available in many different

grades and prices. Good smuggled tea could
be bought for less money, if you didn't mind
that odd little Do-I-smell-a-horse? taste. But
lower even than smuggled tea lurked a nasty
grade of tea: adulterated tea, disgusting and
sometimes downright dangerous. Sometimes
it wasn't even real tea at all.

Housemaids could earn a nice income,
sometimes a shilling a pound, by drying
their employers' soggy used tea leaves and
selling them out the back door to
unscrupulous dealers. The leaves were dyed
to look new and resold to unwary buyers. I
suppose some life may have been left in the
redried tea leaves, but they can't have
provided a stimulating taste experience.

Quality went downhill from there.
Quantities of real tea (new or used) might
be stretched with the addition of other
leaves, twigs, and sometimes floor
sweepings. Even worse, an illegal industry
sprang up to manufacture a type of bogus
tea called "smouch" that never saw China
in its life. According to Richard Twining,
who led the fight against the adulteration of
tea, the fake tea was made with ash tree
leaves that were dried, baked, "trod upon
until the leaves are small, then lifted and
steeped in copperas, with sheep's dung, after
which, being dried on a floor, they are fit for
use." It's worth noting that, sheep's dung
aside, the dyes used on adulterated tea were

[The adulteration of
tea leads to] the
prejudice of the
health of His
Majesty's subjects,
the diminution of the
revenue, the ruin of
the fair trader, and to
the encouragement
of idleness.

— the Tea Adulteration
    Act, 1777

29

often quite poisonous. Copperas is another name for green vitriol, a toxic substance used at that time to make black dye and ink, to tan leather, and to manufacture gunpowder, among its other uses—not exactly what the Austens wanted to drink with their tea.

The British government eventually lowered taxes on tea, but even after the cut in taxes reduced tea prices (which greatly reduced tea smuggling as well), adulteration remained hugely profitable and impossible to stamp out. With such delightfully large profits to be made on bad tea, it paid to be a cautious consumer. Fortunately for the Austens, Jane was a very careful shopper. Let's follow Jane to her reputable dealer, her source of good, pure tea: the tea warehouse of Richard and John Twining.

I am sorry to hear that there has been a rise in tea. I do not mean to pay Twining till later in the day, when we may order a fresh supply.

— Letter from Jane Austen to Cassandra, 6 March 1814

A Visit to Twinings

Jane Austen wrote to Cassandra in 1814 from London, "I am sorry to hear that there has been a rise in tea. I do not mean to pay Twining till later in the day, when we may order a fresh supply." If Jane went in person to fulfill that errand at Twinings tea warehouse, she would have walked through a doorway that looked virtually the same as it does today. The tall doors of 216 The Strand were flanked by classical pillars and topped by an archway with a golden lion and two large, realistically painted Chinese figures (which reminded tea drinkers where their tea had come from). Once inside, she would have been greeted with the aromatic scent of many different sorts of tea. Like many customers of the time, she would probably have smelled the tea to judge its fragrance and character before she bought it.

All tea in those days was bought in bulk and weighed out on apothecaries' scales for the purchaser. Prepackaged tea wasn't produced until 1826, and the tea bag wasn't even dreamt of until the twentieth century. Tea could be bought by the ounce or by the pound, or even by the chest. Jane would have been able to choose from among a dozen or more varieties of tea: black teas such as Bohea, Pekoe, Congou, and Souchong; medium teas such as Imperial and Bing; and green teas such as Hyson and Gunpowder, to name a few. Period mentions of tea often call it either Bohea, meaning black tea, or Hyson, meaning green, but in her works Jane Austen refers to only "tea" and "green tea." It's therefore probable that for her, "tea" meant black tea. Twinings has no record of the kind or amount of tea the Austens ordered from them, but in Jane's letters she once refers to "China Tea," perhaps a type of black tea. The Austens likely bought several pounds at a time, to last until the next opportunity to order from London.

A Delectable Assortment of Treats

Owners of elegant shops, especially those (such as dressmakers and milliners) who catered to women, often offered tea to their customers. It's very probable that Jane Austen was offered tea when she went to such an establishment as Miss Hare's, her milliner in London, to order a pretty new cap ("white sattin and lace, and a little white flower perking out of the left ear"), or to Mrs. Tickars', whose young assistant informed Jane, to her "high amusement, that the stays now are not made to force the Bosom up at all." Tea contributed to the genteel atmosphere of the transaction and paved the way, the shopkeeper hoped, to a pleasant and profitable relationship with the customers. If, on the other hand, Jane went shopping for a bargain, as she often did, to a shop such as Grafton House (where "the whole Counter was thronged, & we waited full half an hour before we c[oul]d be attended to"), she perched on the high stools at the counter, made her choices as quickly as she could, and got out. At such a shop, Jane may have "got her pennyworth for her penny," as Mary Crawford says in *Mansfield Park*, but it was extremely unlikely that she was offered tea.

Should "the miseries of Grafton House" have fatigued her, Jane might have paused in her shopping to rest at a pastrycook's shop. There, she could sit and fan herself while the shopkeeper brought her a tray with a delectable assortment of treats from which to choose. Ices, both water ices and cream ices (that is, ice cream), were popular. "Would you, ma'am, be pleased," the shopkeeper might say, "to take a glass of ice this warm day? Cream-ice, or water-ice, ma'am? Pineapple or strawberry ice?" Buns, queen cakes, tarts, cheesecakes, and jellies were also among the choices available. And, of course, she could always have a refreshing cup of tea. In her letters, Jane Austen mentions a cousin of hers "drinking tea with a Lady" at a pastrycook's shop; and certainly a strawberry ice followed by a steaming pot of tea would be the very thing to polish off a long day's shopping.

She then proceeded to a Pastry-cook's where she devoured six ices, refused to pay for them, knocked down the Pastry Cook & walked away.

— "The Beautifull Cassandra," written by Jane Austen as a young girl

An Ice with Jane Austen

With a fair amount of work, you can recreate some of the goodies with which Jane Austen might have refreshed herself at a pastrycook's shop. If you'd rather not put in the effort after your own long day of shopping, untie a couple of those nice boxes that come from modern pastrycooks' shops and dig some ice cream out of the freezer. Wine or tea to follow—your choice.

Ice Cream

A quart of rich cream.
Half a pound of powdered loaf sugar.
The juice of two large lemons, or a pint of strawberries or raspberries.

Put the cream into a broad pan. Then stir in the sugar by degrees, and when all is well mixed, strain it through a sieve. Put it into a tin that has a close cover, and set it in a tub. Fill the tub with ice broken into very small pieces, and strew among the ice a large quantity of salt, taking care that none of the salt gets into the cream. Scrape the cream down with a spoon as it freezes round the edges of the tin. While the cream is freezing, stir in gradually the lemon-juice, or the juice of a pint of mashed strawberries or raspberries. When it is all frozen, dip the tin in lukewarm water; take out the cream, and fill your glasses; but not till a few minutes before you want to use it, as it will very soon melt.

— *Seventy-five Receipts for Pastry, Cakes, and Sweetmeats*, 1828

This simple and elegant recipe is made essentially the same way today, although a freezer or electric ice cream maker certainly makes the process easier. Recipes of Jane Austen's time generally call for fruit juice strained of its pulp, but adding the mashed fruit in with the juice is nice, too, at least in the case of strawberries.

Strawberry Ice Cream for "The Beautifull Cassandra"

1 quart/ 1 litre/ 4 cups heavy (double) cream or half-and-half
8 oz/ 225 g/ 1-1/2 cups powdered (icing) sugar
Fruit: strained juice of 8 oz/ 225 g/ 2 cups mashed strawberries or raspberries
　　　or juice of two large lemons (approximately 6 tablespoons)

Mix all ingredients; stir well to dissolve sugar. Freeze in a pan in your freezer, scraping and stirring periodically to avoid ice crystals, or in an ice cream maker, following the manufacturer's instructions.

I shall eat Ice & drink French wine, & be above Vulgar Economy.

— Letter from Jane Austen to Cassandra, 2 October 1808

To Make Lemon Cheesecakes

Take the peel of two large lemons, boil it very tender, then pound it well in a mortar, with a quarter of a pound or more of loaf-sugar, the yolks of six eggs, and half a pound of fresh butter, and a little curd beat fine; pound and mix all together, lay a puff paste in your patty-pans, fill them half full and bake them. Orange cheesecakes are done the same way, only you boil the peel in two or three waters, to take out the bitterness.

— *The Art of Cookery Made Plain and Easy, 1796*

Jane Austen's niece Fanny and nephew Edward loved cheesecakes, as she wrote to Cassandra: "Amongst other things we had . . . some cheesecakes on which the children made so delightful a supper as to endear the Town of Devizes to them for a long time." These little cheesecakes are just the right size for a party or for children. Our modern lemons and eggs are probably larger than those of the time, but this recipe seems to work out well anyway. Use organic lemons to avoid dyes and pesticide residues on the peel. I've used full-fat, low-fat, and nonfat cheese with equally good results.

Lemon Cheesecakes for Fanny and Edward

2 large lemons
4 oz/ 110 g/ 1/2 cup white sugar
6 egg yolks
8 oz/ 225 g/ 1 cup unsalted butter
One 15 oz (425 g) container of ricotta cheese, or other light curd cheese
One 17 oz (490 g) package frozen puff pastry, defrosted

Preheat oven to 350°F/ 180°C/ Gas Mark 4

Peel lemons; reserve the pulp and juice for other uses (such as the lemon ice cream, above). Cut the peel into small chunks, boil about 45 minutes or until very tender (use a nonreactive pan, such as stainless steel), then drain. In a food processor, process the lemon peel and sugar until finely ground, add the egg yolks, butter, and cheese, then process until well blended. Cut the puff pastry into circles big enough to line the bottom and sides of your muffin tins and press into the tins. Spoon the cheesecake mixture into the pastry, filling each three-quarters full. Bake until the cheesecakes are puffed and golden and a knife inserted in the center comes out clean (30–40 minutes). Chill. These look pretty garnished with a curl or two of lemon zest. Makes at least 24 muffin-sized cheesecakes.

"That Best of All Travelling Liquors"
Tea Away from Home

"We are to walk about your gardens, and gather the
strawberries ourselves, and sit under trees;—and whatever
else you may like to provide, it is to be all out of doors—a
table spread in the shade, you know. Every thing as natural
and simple as possible."

— Mrs. Elton in *Emma*

Rakes and Courtesans in the Garden

Vauxhall, Ranelagh, White Conduit House, Bagnigge Wells: The names bring to mind images of elegant ladies and gentlemen promenading in formal gardens under trees lit with thousands of gaily colored lanterns. For a shilling or two, which price included tea or coffee, any respectably dressed person could enter a tea garden to walk, talk, listen to concerts, view entertainments, take tea, and, most important, see and be seen. Couples flirted and took tea in covered arbors or lost themselves in shadowy "dark walks," perfect settings for the dishonorable intentions of such rakes as *Pride and Prejudice*'s George Wickham.

At the central rotunda one could enjoy singers who entertained with popular songs, or orchestras that played the compositions of Hayden and Mozart. Fireworks, cascades, and illuminations were popular amusements, as were diversions calculated to amaze the crowds. At some tea gardens, in addition to such expected performers as tumblers, dancers, and conjurers, visitors could see "learned horses," "educated dogs," and spectacles such as the "Exhibition of Bees on Horseback" or the man who promised to "Swallow Phosphorus, Boiling Oil, &c. &c. Without the least inconvenience."

Some tea gardens had begun as pleasure gardens or spas, but when that exotic new beverage, tea, became the fashionable drink of choice, its addition to the fare offered at the gardens contributed greatly to their popularity. Unlike coffee houses, where only men were allowed, tea gardens permitted men and women to enjoy each other's company and tea, too. "The English take a great delight in the public gardens," wrote a Prussian visitor, "where they assemble and drink tea together in the open air."

Come, come, Miss Prissy, make it up, and we will lovers be,
And we will go to Bagnigge Wells, and there will have some tea;
It's there you'll see the lady-birds upon the stinging-nettles,
And there you'll see the waiters, ma'am, with all their shining kettles . . . .
It's there you'll see the waiters, ma'am, will serve you in a trice,
With rolls all hot and butter pats serv'd up so neat and nice

— the 18th-century song "The Prentice to His Mistress"

Though tea gardens were all the rage, opinions about them varied. In Tobias Smollett's *Humphrey Clinker*, Lydia is thrilled by Ranelagh. To her, it looks "like the enchanted palace of a genie . . . crowded with the great, the rich, the gay, the happy, and the fair . . . [They] tread this round of pleasure, or regale . . . with fine imperial tea and other delicious refreshments." Another of Smollett's characters, however, has a sour view: "What are the amusements of Ranelagh? One half of the company are following at the other's tails, in an eternal circle; like so many blind asses in an olive-mill . . . while the other half are drinking hot water, under the denomination of tea, till nine or ten o'clock at night, to keep them awake for the rest of the evening."

There is no evidence that Jane Austen ever visited any of the London tea gardens herself, though she would have read about them in novels such as Smollett's. She mentions tea gardens only twice, in her stories written as a young teenager, and then in a characteristically lampooning fashion. In "Lesley Castle," one food-obsessed woman longs to go to Vauxhall, not to take tea and flirt but "to see whether the cold Beef there is cut so thin as it is reported." In "Catharine," a superficial young lady says she detests another young lady and her family because at Ranelagh "she had such a frightful Cap on, that I have never been able to bear any of them since."

The vogue for gardens to imitate the great London tea gardens spread across Great Britain and to the colonies, with most cities boasting their own miniature "Vauxhalls," as they were nicknamed. Bath, where the Austens visited often, then lived for several years, had its own version: Sydney Gardens. In addition to pleasant garden walks, Sydney Gardens boasted "Water-falls, Pavillions, Alcoves, Grottos, Labyrinth, Bowling-Greens . . . and every requisite that can be conducive to health and pleasure." When the Austens were deciding where in Bath to live, Jane expressed her preference: "It would be very pleasant to be near Sidney Gardens!—we might go into the Labyrinth every day."

Indeed, the Austens ended up settling across the street from the gardens, at No. 4 Sydney Place, which must have delighted Jane. She wrote to Cassandra, "Yesterday was a busy day with me, or at least with my feet & my stockings; I was walking almost all day long; I went to Sydney Gardens soon after one, & did not return till four." Summers offered several grand gala nights, which Jane enjoyed: "There is to be a grand gala on tuesday evening in Sydney Gardens;—a Concert, with Illuminations & fireworks;—to the latter Eliz[abeth] & I look forward with pleasure."

The company at tea gardens was oddly mixed. Courtesans paraded and common "women of the town" trolled for customers along the same walks as their supposedly more respectable clients and their wives. Pickpockets were a common hazard. Some of the *bon ton* found such diverse company exhilarating, but eventually it contributed to tea gardens becoming less fashionable, and, for some of the gardens, less reputable.

Sadly, by the time Jane Austen died in 1817, the days of the tea garden were drawing to a close. First one, then another garden failed and closed its gates for good. It was proof, as if we needed it, that the Victorians didn't appreciate a good time when they saw it. Sydney Gardens in Bath, however, remain open today. No. 4 Sydney Place still stands across the street.

Tea al Fresco

Even at home, the British enjoyed taking their tea "away from home" by drinking it out-of-doors. Most of the great estates in Jane Austen's time included extensive pleasure grounds in addition to their farms and other more mundane areas. There, the owners and their guests could take tea or pass an agreeable hour in the many pleasant walks that wound their way through artistically arranged groves of trees and "shrubberies and flower gardens, and rustic seats innumerable," which Mary Crawford wishes for in *Mansfield Park*.

"He invited us to take our tea in a small summer room, on the brink of a delightful river which rolls its crystal waves along several miles of green enamelled banks; and is the same that passes by the Hermitage."

— Agnes in *Agnes De-Courci*, by Anna Maria Bennett, 1789

Fashions in landscaping had moved away from the rigid symmetry of previous generations. Inspired by landscape painting and the new taste for the romantic in literature, "natural" became the must-have look. Landowners spent huge sums "improving" their estates to fit the new styles. They diverted streams, created lakes, and moved entire hills (and occasionally entire villages) in a display that suggests some estate owners may have had too much time and money on their hands. But when the dirt and debris and unattractive villagers were finally cleared away, the results were admittedly delightful.

Pemberley, Mr. Darcy's estate in *Pride and Prejudice*, is improved, but tastefully. Among other features, "a stream of some natural importance was swelled into greater, but without any artificial appearance. Its banks were neither formal, nor falsely adorned." Elizabeth Bennet (and presumably Jane Austen) approves: "She had never seen a place . . . where natural beauty had been so little counteracted by an awkward taste."

Dim-witted Mr. Rushworth in *Mansfield Park* fusses over how best to bring his estate in line with fashion, and he determines to hire Humphrey Repton, one of the foremost landscape designers of the time, though he will be charged the exorbitant fee of five guineas a day. It is an oddly wise decision, for him. Who can doubt that Mr. Rushworth, left to his own devices, would speedily ruin his estate with "awkward taste"?

The features of these improved landscapes were laid out in a circuit, with the paths cleverly planned to lead strollers along to each new point of interest or scenic view. Classical temples, tea houses, grottoes, hermitages, and artificial ruins fashioned to look as though they had been there forever were carefully placed in a landscape that gave the impression of naturally occurring beauty, though of course there was nothing natural about any of it.

In *Sense and Sensibility*, Marianne Dashwood, mourning in the best sentimental heroine style for the dishonorable Willoughby, steals away "through winding shrubberies" to "a distant eminence; where, from its Grecian temple, her eye, wandering over a wide tract of country to the south-east, could fondly rest on the farthest ridge of hills in the horizon, and fancy that from their summits Combe Magna might be seen."

Guests meandering through the gardens and groves could stop to enjoy each vista or monument, or to chat with the hermit hired specially to live in the hermitage. When tired, they rested on seats "well shaded and sheltered," like Fanny Price's bench in *Mansfield Park*. For refreshment, they might take tea at the tea house or in an arbor. Some landowners even kept small dairies in the pleasure grounds themselves for that purpose. There, at an appropriately quaint cottage, with a cow or two and attendant picturesque milkmaids, visitors could get fresh milk for their tea or a "syllabub from the cow."

In fine weather, people might take their regular evening tea in the tea house, or hold private concerts or other elegant entertainments there, accompanied by tea, ices, and other refreshments. Of course General Tilney, who prides himself on his vast gardens, has a tea house on the grounds of Northanger Abbey. He also has a Hermitage Walk, which no doubt leads to a hermitage. The Bennets in *Pride and Prejudice* have a hermitage as well, though I can't quite imagine General Tilney or even Mrs. Bennet carrying style to the length of hiring hermits to actually live in their gardens.

In *Emma*, the Martins, yeoman farmers, are swept up, too, in the craze for à la mode landscape features. Harriet Smith, who is nothing if not easily impressed, is delighted with their "very handsome summer-house, large enough to hold a dozen people," where "some day next year they were all to drink tea." It's probably not up to General Tilney's standards, but it's a start.

Tea on the Road

By Jane Austen's day, traveling was not nearly the hardship it had been for her grandparents' generation. The main roads were generally much improved by new methods of road building, and most remained passable in all but the worst weather. Off the main highways, travel remained chancier: carriages might be overturned, as happens to the Parkers in *Sanditon*, if they ventured too boldly down a mired or rutted country lane. But at least highwaymen were no longer quite the ever-present danger to purse and health they had been (though Jane's cousin Eliza did claim she was once nearly held up on infamous Hounslow Heath), and travelers blithely set out on long journeys, never doubting they would eventually reach their destinations.

Still, traveling remained an exhausting business. Riding in a carriage was considered exercise, perhaps because it sometimes required real effort to stay in one's seat. Indeed, carriage travel was often a downright bone-jarring

experience, as the nickname of the hired yellow post chaises—"yellow bounders"—suggests. Stagecoaches were particularly uncomfortable, with passengers crammed tightly inside or on top, according to their ability to pay.

Regardless of their mode of transport, travelers often arrived at their destination weary, cold, and feeling rather battered. Jane Austen usually enjoyed her journeys, but Mrs. Austen, like many others, seems not to have borne traveling well—as Jane noted: "My Mother began to suffer from the exercise & fatigue of travelling so far, & she was a good deal indisposed." Often the first (and sometimes the only) refreshment travelers called for upon arriving at their destination was tea, which one author of the time called "that best of all travelling liquors." Jane agreed: "We drank tea as soon as we arrived, & so ends the account of our Journey." A hot drink with a little sugar—just the thing after an exhausting trip.

"I could not tell whether you would be for some meat, or only a dish of tea, after your journey, or else I would have got something ready. . . . Perhaps you would like some tea, as soon as it can be got." They both declared they should prefer it to anything.

— Mrs. Price to Fanny and William in *Mansfield Park*

Tea for the Stranded

Some travelers, unfortunately, did fail to reach their destinations. In the novels that Jane Austen and her contemporaries read, gently bred, refined heroines and heroes regularly find themselves stranded in backwater country villages where the finer things in life are clearly unknown, and where they often have trouble even making themselves understood.

Obviously they require tea, but whether they receive it or not seems to depend on the author's view of country life. Villagers are frequently portrayed either as simple country folk, who are good because they are simple, or as rustic idiots, who are just plain simple. The first are naturally acquainted with tea, as all good people are; the others are either ignorant of tea or openly scornful of such mincing city ways.

The good cottager is portrayed as openly welcoming of weary travelers she has never met before, and understanding of the true noble nature of the heroine or hero, even if she or he is temporarily in distressed circumstances. The woman and her cottage are invariably clean and tidy, and tea is readily available: "The kettle was on the fire, tea-things set, every thing prepared for her guest by the hospitable hostess. . . . The morning sun now came . . . shining across the face of the old woman, as she sat knitting: Lord Colambre thought he had seldom seen a more agreeable countenance . . . [and] benevolent smile." (*The Absentee*, by Maria Edgeworth, 1789.)

The rustic cottager presents a different face to the stranded traveler. She is comically ignorant, and sometimes unhelpful and disrespectful. Typically there is no tea to be had:

Finding that she had no alternative, but that she must remain where she was till the morning, she asked the woman if she could make her a cup of tea?

"Yes, to be sure, I always keeps sage, and balm, and mint, and them sort of herbs?"

"Herbs!" exclaimed Mrs. Freakley; "why, woman, I am not in a fever! I don't want herb tea."

"We never use nothing else here," replied the woman. "I has not got none of that sort like the gentlefolks drinks, as they buys at the shops."

(*Lovers and Friends*, by Anne of Swansea, 1821)

In each novel, tea is used by the author as a sign of character: to know and approve of tea aligns one with civilization, and, by implication, with the good and the right. Those who spurn tea are backward and unenlightened at best; their rejection of it may even be a sign of doubtful morals. It's hard to argue with such logic.

"Feeling myself weary, and my spirits from their unusual exertions, nearly exhausted; I accosted a poor woman, who was placing her spinning-wheel at the door of a hut, that could hardly be distinguished by the name of house; I entreated she would suffer me to rest, and get me a dish of tea."

— Agnes in *Agnes De-Courci*, by Anna Maria Bennett, 1789

In Mrs. La Tournelle's Parlor

When Jane Austen was ten years old, she and Cassandra, who was twelve, spent a year and a half at the Reading Ladies Boarding School. It was probably the inspiration for Mrs. Goddard's "real, honest, old-fashioned Boarding school," which Harriet Smith attends in *Emma*. Like Harriet, the Austen sisters held the special status of "parlor boarder," for which Mr. Austen paid £35 a year for each girl, more than double what ordinary boarders were charged.

Parlor boarders ate their breakfast and dinner with the other girls in the schoolroom, but, among other privileges, they took their tea and supper with the owner of the school, Mrs. La Tournelle. It's an interesting picture: the Austen girls and the other favored students cozily drinking tea in front of the fire in Mrs. La Tournelle's parlor, "hung round with fancy-work" like Mrs. Goddard's, while the less fortunate pupils were left to their apparently tea-less existence in the schoolroom. With Mrs. La Tournelle, Jane and the other parlor boarders could imitate the elegance to which they were accustomed at home: graceful little tea tables, china cups and teapots, muffins, cake, dainty slices of bread and butter, and adult conversation.

Though respectable and well-connected socially, Mrs. La Tournelle was not a particularly refined or educated woman. She must nevertheless have been fascinating to Jane: She had a cork leg of mysterious origins, and a large fund of stories (of equally mysterious origins) about actors and the behind-the-scenes life of the theater that she was fond of sharing whenever she got the chance. I like to picture ten-year-old Jane sitting attentively, drinking in

> The letter which I have this moment received from you has diverted me beyond moderation. I could die of laughter at it, as they used to say at school.

— Letter from Jane Austen to her sister, Cassandra, 1 September 1796

inspiration for her future writings along with her tea.

Two of Jane Austen's brothers, Frank and Charles, also went away to school, attending the Royal Naval Academy in Portsmouth in preparation for their future careers in the navy. At the academy they took lessons not only in navigation and gunnery, but also in French, drawing, and dancing, accomplishments appropriate for young men of good family. We know Mr. Austen gave them an allowance liberal enough to enable them to drink tea, because a former schoolmate later wrote to Charles reminiscing about their daily "evening tea party." This all sounds innocent and refined enough, until we notice that the schoolmate underlined the phrase. Perhaps the teenaged students of the Academy were spiking their tea with a little something to add liveliness to the evening?

Tea and Grog

It was not to be expected that an officer in His Majesty's Royal Navy, being used to tea at least twice a day at home, would give up the habit once at sea. Indeed, for officers, life aboard ship included most of the comforts of home, as Jane Austen knew from her sailor brothers, Frank and Charles. She frequently drew on their personal experiences for the descriptions of navy life in her novels.

In *Persuasion*, Captain Wentworth explains to the Miss Musgroves how civilized life on board can be, which reminds Anne Elliot "of the early days when she too had been ignorant, and she too had been accused of supposing sailors to be living on board without anything to eat, or any cook to dress it if there were, or any servant to wait, or any knife and fork to use." A refined man such as Captain Wentworth would naturally expect to drink tea on board, just as he did ashore. Beer, wine, and grog all had their merits and their place at the officers' mess, but for a British gentleman they were no substitute for tea.

Unfortunately, the navy did not provide tea. The rations did include such homely fare as pickled meats, dried peas, and oatmeal, as well as a daily allotment of a gallon of beer or other liquor, but officers had to bring their own tea. Most chose to bring their own food stores as well, pooling their resources to produce meals they considered fit for gentlemen. They even brought goats on board with the other livestock, to provide a reliable source of milk for their tea.

Captain Wentworth's sister often goes to sea with her admiral husband and apparently finds life aboard ship congenial: "'I do assure you, ma'am,' pursued Mrs. Croft, 'that nothing can exceed the accommodations of a man of war; I speak, you know, of the higher rates. When you come to a frigate, of course, you are more confined—though any reasonable woman may be perfectly happy in one of them; and I can safely say, that the happiest part of my life has been spent on board a ship.'" Clearly Mrs. Croft never had to do without her tea at sea.

The Admiral says, "Come, sit down and have a glass of grog. . . . I breakfast at eight, dine at three, have tea in the evening, and grog at night, as you see."

— Captain Harry Smith, 1814

Officers and Gentlemen

Many army and militia officers managed to live a fashionable life, which of course included tea, even during active service. When stationed at one place for some time, as were the militia officers in *Pride and Prejudice*, they found it fairly easy to live the normal life of a British gentleman. Under such circumstances, some officers brought their wives and families with them; they lived in private quarters and generally conducted themselves as if they were at home. Being on maneuvers made things more difficult, but even so, certain standards were kept. Officers were allowed to keep servants and bring private stores and baggage with them. As long as the baggage train could keep up with the troops and they were involved in no fighting, meals and tea could be easily produced when camp was made. Captain John Kincaid of the 95th Rifle Brigade understood the importance of tea on maneuvers: "If it is early in the day, the first thing to be done is to make some tea, the most sovereign restorative for jaded spirits. We then proceed to our various duties."

The army had its camp followers, as any army does: women who traveled with the soldiers and provided washing, cooking, and other more particular services for the common soldier. Some officers' wives also accompanied their husbands from post to post, as Colonel Forster's wife does in *Pride and Prejudice*. The Duke of Wellington saw both camp followers and officers' wives as encumbrances that greatly slowed the movement of his troops, and indeed an officer moving his household could present a laughably awkward picture. A prisoner, Frenchman Baron Lejeune, described a British captain's household on the move: "Then came his wife, in a pretty costume . . . seated on a mule . . . whilst she led by a blue ribbon a tame goat, which was to supply her night and morning with cream for her cup of tea." The family's baby and its nurse and other servants came next, then "a donkey laden with the voluminous baggage of the family, surmounted by a tea-kettle and cage full of canaries."

Even under the most extreme circumstances, an officer would contrive to have with him at least a little tea. When involved in active fighting, an officer had only the contents of his haversack to depend on. Captain Kincaid maintained that a well-regulated haversack "ought never to be without the following . . . viz. a couple of biscuits, a sausage, a little tea and sugar, a knife, fork, and spoon, a tin cup, (which answers to the names of tea-cup, soup-plate, wine-glass, and tumbler,) a pair of socks, a piece of soap, a tooth-brush, towel, and comb, and half a dozen cigars."

After the British victory at Waterloo, dashing Major Harry Smith, understandably exhausted, had nothing available to eat or drink except tea: "I had some tea in my writing-case, but no sugar. It had been carried by an orderly, although in the ranks. He found me out after the battle, and I made some tea in a soldier's tin." He and some other officers rested and drank their tea, a fitting end to the greatest battle of the Napoleonic wars.

BATTLE OF WATERLOO, 18th June, 1815. When I awoke this morning at daylight I found myself drenched with rain. …We made a fire…and boiled a huge campkettle full of tea, mixed up with a suitable quantity of milk and sugar, for breakfast; and as it stood on the edge of the high road where all the big-wigs of the army had occasion to pass in the early part of the morning, I believe almost every one of them, from the Duke downwards, claimed a cupful.

— *Adventures in the Rifle Brigade*, by Captain John Kincaid, 1830

Emma's Box Hill Picnic and Captain Wentworth's Mess

To Make a Syllabub from the Cow

Make your syllabub of either cyder or wine, sweeten it pretty sweet, and grate nutmeg in; then milk the milk into the liquor: when this is done, pour over the top half a pint or pint of cream, according to the quantity of syllabub you make. You may make this syllabub at home, only have new milk; make it as hot as milk from the cow, and out of a tea-pot, or any such thing, pour it in, holding your hand very high, and strew over some currants well washed and picked, and plumped before the fire.

—*The Art of Cookery Made Plain and Easy*, 1796

First, catch your cow. . . . If you haven't a cow in your back yard, you can try the recipe's second option. The interesting texture of this syllabub comes from the fact that the wine or other acidic liquid curdles the milk when they are mixed together, so if you use a substitute for the wine or cider, it must have an acidic component, such as lemon juice. Unhomogenized (but still pasteurized) milk is closest to what Jane Austen would have used, and is best for this recipe, as it curdles and whips up more easily than homogenized milk. It is sometimes available at health food stores, although if you can't find it locally you could try replacing one-fourth to one-third the volume of milk with heavy cream.

The amount of liquor and milk to use is more problematic. A recipe from *The London Art of Cookery* calls for "a pint of cyder and a bottle of strong beer" and "as much milk as will make a strong froth," which was a bit hard for me to pin down, not having a prior acquaintance with cows and their froth-making capabilities. I ended up using a proportion of two parts milk to one part liquor, which seemed satisfactory.

This brings us to the next point: How hot, exactly, is "as hot as milk from the cow"? I am reliably informed by veterinary sources that "normal cow body core temperature" is 101.5°F (38.6°C). You can heat the milk gently in a microwave oven or over low heat on the stove, using a candy or meat thermometer to check the temperature. I used a plastic squeezable sports bottle to squirt the milk into the cider. Whisking or mixing the syllabub helps break down the curds that form and gives it a pleasanter texture.

For a lighter, more dessert-like syllabub, see "Recipes for a Grand Entertainment."

A Syllabub (Indirectly) from the Cow

1 pint/ 1/2 litre/ 2 cups hard cider, wine, or lemonade, room temperature
3 tablespoons powdered (icing) sugar (more or less according to your sweet tooth)
1/4 nutmeg, grated (or 1/2 teaspoon ground nutmeg)
1 quart/ 1 litre/ 4 cups whole, unhomogenized (but pasteurized) milk, heated to approximately 101.5°F/ 38.6°C
4 tablespoons dried currants, soaked in warm water until plump

Pour the cider or wine into a large punch bowl or mixing bowl. Add the sugar and nutmeg and stir to dissolve. Pour or squirt the milk into the cider and stir, then whisk or mix with an electric mixer until smooth. Sprinkle with currants. Serve with tea in your tea house.

For Captains of Ships
To Make Catchup to Keep Twenty Years

Take a gallon of strong stale beer, one pound of anchovies washed from the pickle, a pound of shalots peeled, half an ounce of mace, half an ounce of cloves, a quarter of an ounce of whole pepper, three or four large races of ginger, two quarts of the large mushroom-flaps rubbed to pieces; cover all this close, and let it simmer till it is half wasted, then strain it through a flannel bag; let it stand till it is quite cold, then bottle it. You may carry it to the Indies. A spoonful of this to a pound of fresh butter melted makes a fine fish-sauce, or in the room of gravy sauce. The stronger and staler the beer is, the better the catchup will be.

— *The Art of Cookery Made Plain and Easy*, 1796

This recipe looks just completely awful at first glance, but on closer inspection it appears to be a species of Worcestershire sauce (the ingredients of which should not be closely examined, anyway). Mrs. Austen may well have put up this sauce or followed such similarly useful recipes as "To make Fish-Sauce to keep the whole Year" and "To pickle Mushrooms for the Sea" for her sailor sons. You may feel up to attempting a modern version of this ketchup recipe, but I plan to buy mine at the store.

"The tea!—the tea!—the wholesome tea!"

Tea and Health

The tea!—the tea!—the wholesome tea!
The black, the green, the mix'd, the good, the strong Bohea!...
For it's good for the nerves, and warms my heart,
And from it I will never part ...
And death, whenever he comes to me,
Will find me—drinking a good strong cup of tea.

— from the early 19th-century song, "The Tea"

As to Beauty . . . Tea increases the Quantity of Bile in too frequent Drinkers of it. Now what Physicians call Bile . . . Dries up, and shrivels their Skin. And thereby brings Wrinkles on Women's Faces, long before Age does. Hence Physicians call Bile the Mother of Deformity, and Nothing increases Bile more in Women's Faces, than too Frequent Drinking of Tea. So that if Women would but drink Less Tea, they would preserve their Beauty.

— "Farther Observations on the Ill Effects of [tea] by a learned Physician," 1737

Tempest in a Teapot

Tea provoked a stormy debate from the moment it first arrived in Europe in the early 1600s. Like many new foods and beverages, it was first hailed by some physicians as a cure-all, good for everything from headaches to gout to bubonic plague. This, of course, provoked rival physicians, who, not content with denying tea's benefits, declared it to be a pernicious poison. Tea lingered for a while as a medicinal herb, sold only in small quantities by apothecaries, but then started to become fashionable. Tea's pleasant effects, exotic origins, and extraordinarily high cost at first— which meant that only the rich could drink it—soon raised it to the heights of stylishness and took it forever out of the hands of mere medical men, though sellers of tea continued to puff up its medical virtues to help sales. In 1660, Thomas Garway, in one of the earliest known tea advertisements, declared that tea was "most wholesome, preserving in perfect health untill extreme Old Age."

Among its many "Vertues and Excellencies" were its benefits, he claimed, for the kidneys, liver, digestion, fevers, dropsy, and scurvy; and, probably more to the point, "It overcometh superfluous Sleep, and prevents Sleepiness in general."

Some Britons viewed tea's growing popularity with disfavor, sneering at it as unmanly, untraditional, and un-British. Brewers were especially alarmed by the new beverage. By the mid-1700s tea was threatening to replace ale and beer on British tables. Fearing loss of sales, brewers tried to drum up opposition to tea, even lobbying the government to raise taxes on it. One particularly indignant fellow wrote a furious letter to *Gentleman's Magazine*, claiming tea caused feebleness, cowardice, poor blood, barren women, and dissatisfied servants. He topped off his diatribe with an objection to how tea was taken: "Were it entirely wholesome as Balm or Mint, it were yet Mischief enough to have our whole Populace used to sip warm Water in a mincing effeminate Manner once or twice a Day; which hot Water must be supped out of a nice Tea-cup, sweetened with Sugar, biting a Bit of nice thin Bread and Butter between whiles." Perhaps he was a brewer.

The debate over tea has continued in one form or another until the present day, when science seems finally to have proved that tea is, after all, as one poet called it, "the sovereign drink of pleasure and of health."

The Apothecary's Arsenal

Though it had become clear by Jane Austen's day that tea would not cure bubonic plague, it was still thought (except by its detractors) to have some medical benefits. In addition to its undeniably useful ability to lift the fog of a hangover, green tea leaves could be chewed for heartburn—both convenient qualities in an age of excessive indulgence at the table. Tea was also classed with mineral water by some physicians as being capable of removing "obstruction" (that is, aiding the flow of fluids in the body), probably because of its mild diuretic properties. Keeping the body free of

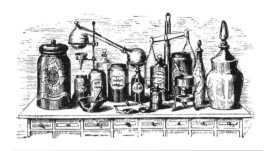

Henry is an excellent Patient, lies quietly in bed & is ready to swallow anything. He lives upon Medicine, Tea & Barley water.

— Letter from Jane Austen to her sister, Cassandra, 18 October 1815

obstruction was a major preoccupation for eighteenth century physicians. Unfortunately, some of the medicines they used, unlike tea, were extremely poisonous, and their doctoring methods seemed as likely to kill as to cure the patient. Many medical men of the time favored so-called "heroic medicine": aggressive blood-letting, vomiting, intestinal purging, sweating, and blistering.

When Jane Austen's brother Henry fell slightly ill with a "bilious attack," his apothecary (they were often called in place of physicians) gave him calomel—a harsh, mercury-based laxative guaranteed to clean out a patient and poison him to boot. The apothecary then bled him at least three days running: twenty ounces of blood a day, amounting to almost four pints—roughly one-third to one-half the blood a human body contains. Not surprisingly, Henry became dangerously ill. He did recover, amazingly enough, considering that his apothecary continued to treat him. Perhaps it was due to Jane's careful nursing and tea. The wonder is he had the strength to drink it.

Herbs and Dandelions

By Jane Austen's time, tea was such an important part of life that people tended to call all leaf infusions "tea," whether or not they contained any real tea leaves. For centuries the British had drunk herbal infusions (which went by the name "tisanes"), but with the coming of Chinese tea they happily discarded the old name, and everything became "tea." People drank teas made from such common garden herbs as mint, chamomile, and lemon balm, as we still do today, as well as teas from other garden herbs now less often made into teas, such as sage (good for "apoplexy, epilepsy, palsy and trembling of the limbs"), thyme ("an excellent remedy for headaches and giddiness" and "that troublesome disease the nightmare"), marjoram (for asthma or cough), and lavender ("good in catarrhs [runny nose], apoplexy, palsy, spasms, vertigo").

People also made teas from many other plants that sound more medicinal and less pleasant, such as colt's foot (good for "consumption" [tuberculosis] and "to cleanse humours"), St. John's wort ("good in the jaundice"), and pennyroyal (for "the gravel" [kidney stones]). It's interesting to note that herbalists today still prescribe some of the same herbs for the same conditions, though fortunately we've discovered more effective remedies for tuberculosis than colt's foot tea.

In Jane Austen's unfinished novel *Sanditon*, the Miss Parkers drink herbal tea, probably the least harmful of all the ways they doctor themselves. In real life, Jane's mother

Then they will settle about the Dandelion Tea;—the receipts for which were shewn him at Basingstoke, & he approved of them highly; they will only require some slight alteration to be better adapted to my Mother's Constitution.

— Letter from Jane Austen to Cassandra, 27 October 1798

drank dandelion tea, almost certainly prescribed for her "bilious complaints"—that is, for her liver and her digestive difficulties, which she seems to have suffered from often. But then, she suffered (or thought she did) from a lot. Jane was apparently somewhat skeptical and less than sympathetic about Mrs. Austen's complaints. "My Mother continues hearty," she once wrote to Cassandra, "her appetite & nights are very good, but her Bowels are still not entirely settled, & she sometimes complains of an Asthma, a Dropsy, Water in her Chest & a Liver Disorder." Another time she wrote: "She is tolerably well. . . . She would tell you herself that she has a very dreadful cold in her head at present; but I have not much compassion for colds in the head without fever or sore throat." At any rate, Mrs. Austen was probably kept happy with her dandelion tea, a medicine that is still prescribed by herbalists today for good digestion and cleansing of the liver. It was certainly less harmful than some of the outright poisonous medicines she could have been taking, and it may even have helped—she outlived her daughter Jane by ten years.

Tea and the Delicate Constitution

The novels of Jane Austen's time were full of Languishing Heroines. Ethereal, probably consumptive, young women, they appeared to live upon their nerves, perhaps a morsel of toast, and, of course, tea. No self-respecting young lady in love would eat: "I have cried without ceasing, and have not tasted any thing but tea," wails Lydia Melford in Tobias Smollett's *Humphrey Clinker*.

Jane Austen enjoyed poking fun at such characters in her own novels. In *Sense and Sensibility*, Marianne Dashwood, who reads a great deal, knows what is expected of a young woman of delicate sensibilities: "Marianne would have thought herself very inexcusable had she been able to sleep at all the first night after parting from Willoughby. . . . She was awake the whole night, and she wept the greatest part of it. She got up with a headache, was unable to talk, and unwilling to take any nourishment; . . . Her sensibility was potent enough!" Despite her emotional state, she nevertheless drinks her tea: "Elinor now began to make the tea, and Marianne was obliged to appear again."

Jane Austen herself had not much sympathy for the lovelorn. Writing to a niece who had decided that she was not, after all, in love, she said, "It is no creed of mine, as you must be well aware, that such sort of Disappointments kill anybody."

For every delicate young lady who subsisted solely on tea and poetry, there were others, even more fragile, whose nerves were too brittle even for the gentle tonic of tea. In *Sanditon*, Diana, Susan, and Arthur Parker are either unfortunate invalids or dreadful hypochondriacs,

"I am very sorry to hear, Miss Fairfax, of your being out this morning in the rain. Young ladies should take care of themselves.—Young ladies are delicate plants."

— Mr. Woodhouse in *Emma*

depending on one's point of view. When Charlotte Heywood visits them for tea, she is amazed to see that the tea tray has "almost as many Teapots &c as there were persons in company." Diana and Susan each drink a different sort of medicinal herb tea. Arthur indulges himself with rich, strong cocoa rather than tea because he fancies himself nervous. A rather stout young man, he sweats heavily at the least exercise, and insists "there cannot be a surer sign of Nervousness."

For the guests there is normal green tea, which Charlotte, of course, enjoys. Arthur is astonished:

> "What!" said he—"Do you venture upon two dishes of strong
> Green Tea in one Even[in]g?—What Nerves you must have!—
> How I envy you.—Now, if I were to swallow only one such
> dish—what do you think it's [sic] effect would be upon me?—
> "Keep you awake perhaps all night"—replied Charlotte. . . .
> "Oh! if that were all!"—he exclaimed.—"No—it acts on me
> like Poison and w[oul]d entirely take away the use of my right
> side, before I had swallowed it 5 minutes."

Tea's stimulating qualities were well known, but it had become such a pervasive part of British life that it did not always occur to people that their difficulties in sleeping might lie in their after-dinner tea. Jane Austen wrote to Cassandra to recommend that a friend of theirs give up tea: "Have you ever mentioned the leaving off Tea to Mrs K.?—Eliza has just spoken of it again.— The Benefit *she* has found from it in sleeping, has been very great." Jane's love of tea didn't seem to affect *her* sleep: "We went to bed at 10. I was very tired, but slept to a miracle & am lovely today."

Tea for Oppressed Heroines

Another common theme in the novels that Jane Austen so loved to lampoon is that of the Abducted Heroine. The young lady, no doubt an heiress, is typically spirited away by a scoundrel with designs on her virtue. This plight is satirically described by Jane Austen in *Northanger Abbey*: The villain is assisted by three men "in horsemen's greatcoats, by whom she will hereafter

The old woman pressed her to take something, till she at length consented to take one cup of tea, which was brought. Maria now finding herself alone, gave vent to her feelings. . . . "No," cried she, in a louder tone, "he may keep me a prisoner for life, he may kill me, but never will I be his."

— *Simple Facts*, by Mrs. Matthews, 1793

be forced into a traveling-chaise and four, which will drive off with incredible speed."

The oppressed heroine, confined to rough quarters with only a slatternly servant loyal to her abductor, usually refuses all nourishment in protest, except—a cup of tea. Food is too crude, too physical, too at odds with her sublime, spiritual nature, but tea suits her sensitive, refined temperament. That she takes tea from the hands of the villain shows that even a noble heroine has her limits. Indeed, tea seems the only thing that preserves her delicate health, allowing her to live, to carry on, to survive her numerous fainting fits, and, in the end, to triumph over her persecutor. The moral is clear: deprive a British lady of her freedom, her honor, and her life, but don't deprive her of her tea.

Spiritual Refreshment and Inspiration

Jane Austen understood well the refreshing, comforting qualities of tea. In *Sense and Sensibility*, when Marianne Dashwood barely survives a dangerous illness, her sister Elinor, who has watched and nursed her through the crisis, turns with relief to tea: "At seven o'clock, leaving Marianne still sweetly asleep, she joined Mrs. Jennings in the drawing-room to tea. Of breakfast she had been kept by her fears, and of dinner by their sudden reverse, from eating much;—and the present refreshment, therefore, with such feelings of

*The Muse's friend,
tea does our fancy aid,
Repress those vapours
which the head invade,
And keeps the palace of
the soul serene*

— late 17th-century poem
"Of Tea," by
Edmund Waller

content as she brought to it, was particularly welcome."

Tea was useful in cases of emotional distress, as well. In *Northanger Abbey*, Catherine Morland is sent home abruptly from the dreadful General Tilney's house. The first thing her mother does, noticing Catherine's "pale and jaded looks," is to order tea for her. In *Mansfield Park*, Fanny Price, returning home after an exhausting journey, is grateful for the tea prepared by her thoughtful sister: "Fanny's spirit was as much refreshed as her body; her head and heart were soon the better for such well-timed kindness."

Tea could also assist literary inspiration. One of Jane Austen's favorite authors, Samuel Johnson—her "dear Dr. Johnson," as she called him—was completely mad about tea. Brilliant and wickedly amusing, he described himself as "a hardened and shameless tea-drinker, who has for twenty years diluted his meals with only the infusion of this fascinating plant; whose kettle has scarcely time to cool; who with tea amuses the evening, with tea solaces the midnight, and with tea welcomes the morning." Known to drink fifteen cups at a sitting, he wrote prolifically, often late into the night, kept awake by tea. Samuel Johnson and Jane Austen were both brilliant writers and they both loved tea. A mere coincidence? I think not.

Tea with That Little Something Extra

If tea by itself didn't provide enough refreshment and inspiration, it could always be helped along with a little slosh of something more stimulating. Gentlemen (and some ladies) were known to spike their tea, sometimes even at breakfast, though that may have had a hair-of-the-dog quality to it. After dinner, when the ladies retired to the drawing room, the gentlemen customarily sat over their wine in the dining room, sometimes for hours. The men of the Georgian and Regency periods routinely drank quantities of alcohol that seem staggering today, often several bottles of wine each at a sitting. When finally called to join the ladies for tea, topping off their teacups with spirits probably seemed like the natural thing to do.

> She was silent and cross during the remainder of the evening; and the next morning, at breakfast, she was so low that even her accustomed dose of brandy, in her tea, had no effect.
>
> — *"The Lottery,"* by Maria Edgeworth, 1804

If spiked tea brought on unpleasant symptoms, plain tea provided the cure. In *The Loiterer*, the college newspaper written mostly by Jane Austen's brothers James and Henry, the spoof "Diary of a Modern Oxford Man" points out the usefulness of tea as a pick-me-up the morning after a bender: "Went to the Angel and dined—famous evening till eleven . . . eleven to one, went down into St. Thomas's and fought a raff—one, dragged home by somebody, the Lord know whom, and put to bed. . . . Very bruised and sore, did not get up till twelve . . . drank six dishes of tea—did not know what to do with myself, so wrote to my father for money."

Proper Nourishment for the Sick

To Make Water-Gruel

You must take a pint of water and a large spoonful of oatmeal; then stir it together and let it boil up three or four times, stirring it often; do not let it boil over; then strain it through a sieve, salt it to your palate, put in a good piece of fresh butter, brew it with a spoon till the butter is all melted, then it will be fine and smooth, and very good: some love a little pepper in it.

— *The Art of Cookery Made Plain and Easy*, 1796

"You must go to bed early, my dear—and I recommend a little gruel to you before you go.—You and I will have a nice basin of gruel together." In *Emma*, Mr. Woodhouse loves his gruel, but it has to be made just so. It must be "nice smooth gruel, thin, but not too thin." Let's hope that this recipe would meet with his approval. I've drawn from recipes from several period cookbooks for hints about how to proceed. Water gruel is a versatile recipe. Salt and sugar appear in most recipes; flavorings vary according to preference.

Water Gruel for Mr. Woodhouse

16 fl oz/ 1/2 litre/ 2 cups water

3 tablespoons quick-cooking (coarsely ground) oatmeal

Salt as desired

Sugar to taste

1 tablespoon butter

Flavorings: pepper to taste, *or*

   nutmeg and/or wine, sherry, or port (or spirits, recommended for a cold), *or*

   a cinnamon stick or a bit of lemon peel boiled with the oatmeal, *or*

   1–2 teaspoons lemon juice squeezed into the finished gruel

Bring the water to a boil; gradually stir in the oatmeal. Add the lemon peel or cinnamon stick, if used, at this point. Let the mixture boil gently, about 5 minutes, stirring often. Then strain it through a colander to catch any big bits—this is supposed to be a drink, more or less. Add the butter and sugar to the liquid, and stir until smooth. Stir in any desired flavorings. Serve warm in a basin (à la Mr. Woodhouse) or in a cup. Makes 1 large serving.

Though it is not our intention to invade the province of the physician or apothecary, that being totally foreign to the plan of a work of this kind, yet it is certainly the indispensable duty of every housekeeper, to know how properly to provide every kind of kitchen nourishment for the sick.

— *The London Art of Cookery,* 1807

Barley Water

Boil a quarter of a pound of pearl barley in two quarts of water, skim it very clean, and when it has boiled half away, strain it. Make it moderately sweet, and put in two spoonfuls of white wine. It must be made a little warm before you drink it.

— *The London Art of Cookery*, 1807

Barley water is a pleasant, mildly sweet drink. I can see why Henry Austen liked it when he was ill. King George III preferred it to wine after a hard day's hunting, which greatly incensed his gentlemen-in-waiting. (Mind you, this may have been a sign of his approaching madness.) Some recipes call for lemon juice, if you prefer it to wine.

Barley Water for Henry Austen and King George

4 oz/ 110 g/ scant 2/3 cup pearled barley
2 quarts/ 2 litres/ 8 cups water
4 oz/ 110 g/ 1/2 cup sugar, or more to taste
2 fl oz/ 60 ml/ 1/4 cup white wine or lemon juice

Bring the water to a boil, using a large pot. Stir in the barley. Simmer very gently, covered, over low heat, for about 2 hours. Strain the liquid into a bowl—you should have 4–5 cups (a little over 1 litre) of liquid; if not, add more water to make up the amount. Reserve the barley grains for another use. (Barley makes a nice pudding, similar to rice pudding.) Stir in the sugar until it dissolves. Add the wine or lemon juice. Serve warm or chilled. Makes 4–5 servings.

To Make China Orange Jelly

To two ounces of isinglass, boiled down very strong by itself, put one quart of orange-juice, with a little cinnamon, mace, as much sugar as you require, the whites of eight eggs. Boil all together about ten minutes pretty fast, run it through a bag; and after it is cleared, take some of the skin of the orange, cut small like straws, and put into it. N.B. it is a great improvement to add the juice of two Seville oranges.

— *The Art of Cookery Made Plain and Easy, 1796*

In *Mansfield Park*, Mrs. Norris makes off with all the leftover jellies from Fanny Price's ball, supposedly for her sick maid. Knowing Mrs. Norris, it seems unlikely that her maid ever saw them. Jellies (which are similar to our modern gelatin desserts) are pleasant little trifles, fit for a ball or a patient. The following recipe is one of the easiest versions to make.

Isinglass is gelatin made from fish. It may be available at wine-making shops, but regular unflavored gelatin is easier to find. The egg whites were used to clarify the jelly, as was the jelly bag. The jelly won't be as clear without using a bag, but it's much less troublesome and just as tasty if you choose to run the mixture through a fine mesh strainer. Seville oranges are bitter oranges, much used in the making of marmalade.

China Orange Jelly for Mrs. Norris's Maid
3 tablespoons granulated gelatin
4 oz/ 110 g/ 1/2 cup white sugar, or more to taste
8 fl oz/ 225 g/ 1 cup boiling water
1 quart/ 1 litre/ 4 cups orange juice, strained of pulp
1/8 teaspoon each cinnamon and mace
Very fine parings of orange zest (optional)

Dissolve the gelatin and sugar in the boiling water, stirring until completely dissolved (about 5 minutes). Stir in the orange juice and spices, then strain the mixture through a jelly bag or a fine mesh strainer. Chill until just slightly thickened (no more than an hour), then fold in the orange zest. Pour the mixture into a mold or individual dishes. Chill 6 hours or until completely set.

"You must drink tea with us tonight"
Tea in the Evening

The Tea things were brought in.—"Oh! my dear Mrs Parker
—you should not indeed—why would you do so? I was just
upon the point of wishing you good Evening. But since you
are so very neighbourly, I believe Miss Clara & I must stay."

— Lady Denham in *Sanditon*

At the End of the Day

The end of the day in Jane Austen's era was a special, welcome time when family and friends gathered together after the day's activities. The gentlemen returned home when their business was done and the ladies left off their work around the house (though for some, such as the indolent Lady Bertram in *Mansfield Park*, work and relaxation were admittedly indistinguishable). They met for dinner, then assembled later in the drawing room to take tea and spend the evening entertaining one another. Tea provided an excuse to come together and socialize. Jane's "dear Dr. Johnson" called it "a pretence for assembling to prattle, for interrupting business, or diversifying idleness. They, who drink one cup, and [they], who drink twenty, are equally punctual in preparing or partaking it . . . they are brought together not by the tea, but the teatable."

> The next opening of the door brought something more welcome; it was for the tea-things, which she had begun almost to despair of seeing that evening.
>
> — *Mansfield Park*

At what time people took their evening tea was a matter of personal preference. Because it generally followed the end of dinner by one or two hours, teatime depended on when dinner was eaten. When Jane Austen's parents were young, dining in the early to middle afternoon was usual. People of fashion, to distinguish themselves from the common folk, dined later, perhaps three or four o'clock. Naturally, aspiring ladies and gentlemen changed their hours to imitate high society, which responded by pushing the dinner hour even later. A little dance ensued, with the upper classes and the stylish retreating from the dreadful fate of being thought common, and the would-be fashionable following as fast as they could. By the Regency period the modish were dining at six o'clock, seven o'clock, and later.

Especially in the countryside, the old-fashioned and those with no pretensions to fashion continued to keep early dinner hours, a fact that Jane Austen used to highlight social differences in her novels. In *Pride and Prejudice*, Bingley's snobbish sisters, who have a horror of anything vulgar or provincial, no doubt set the dinner hour of half-past six at their brother's house. The Bennets dine some two hours earlier, a practice that must add to the contempt the sisters feel for them. In her unfinished novel *The Watsons*, Jane Austen portrays the Watsons as eating their dinner at three, but at the Castle, Lord Osborne and his guests "are but just rising from dinner at midnight," an exaggeration designed to show how extremely stylish they are.

The Austens themselves altered their dinner time over the years as the fashion changed. In 1798 Jane jokingly wrote to Cassandra (who was staying at their wealthy brother's house), "We dine now at half after Three, & have done dinner I suppose before you begin—We drink tea at half after six.—I am afraid you will despise us." But in 1808 she noted that "we never dine now till five," an almost stylish hour, though I doubt it would have impressed Bingley's sisters.

The modern practice of taking "afternoon tea" before dinner would probably have struck Jane Austen and her contemporaries as odd. In her era, tea was always served *after* dinner (though when dinner was eaten early enough, teatime may still have fallen during what we call the afternoon). Confusing the issue further is that people of the time referred to all hours before dinner as "morning," and the period between dinner and tea as "afternoon," even if it fell in what we now call the evening. To them, "evening" started after tea. The institution of afternoon tea is a Victorian invention, created in response to the ever-later dinner hours. History usually credits Anna, seventh Duchess of Bedford, with originating the custom of afternoon tea around 1840. Complaining that she felt "a sinking feeling" in the late afternoon, she began to take tea and eat a few tidbits in her boudoir at five o'clock. She often invited select friends to join her, and these fashionable ladies helped to popularize the custom.

Waiting for Tea

The custom in England during the Georgian and Regency periods (and indeed well into our time) was for the ladies to withdraw after dinner. The gentlemen lingered in the dining room, indulging in wine and presumably in free and easy male conversation. In the drawing room, the ladies talked, read, or worked on stitchery to pass the time until the men joined them, after an hour or so, for tea. Cartoons and novels of the time sometimes show a different reality, of the men staggering in drunk after two or three hours, only to complain that the tea was cold.

Jane Austen knew how tedious the interval between dinner and tea could be. While the female guests in *Pride and Prejudice* wait for the men after dinner at Lady Catherine de Bourgh's, "there was little to be done but to hear Lady Catherine talk, which she did without any intermission." In *Sense and*

Anxious and uneasy, the period which passed in the drawing-room, before the gentlemen came, was wearisome and dull to a degree, that almost made her uncivil. She looked forward to their entrance, as the point on which all her chance of pleasure for the evening must depend. "If he does not come to me, *then*," said she, "I shall give him up for ever."

— Elizabeth Bennet in *Pride and Prejudice*

Sensibility, conversation at John and Fanny Dashwood's house is numbingly boring during dinner, but afterward is worse: "When the ladies withdrew to the drawing-room after dinner, this poverty was particularly evident, for the gentlemen *had* supplied the discourse with some variety—the variety of politics, inclosing land, and breaking horses." The only topic of conversation for the ladies is provided by young Harry Dashwood, who has probably been allowed to join the adults for dessert and tea, as children of the time often did even when guests were present. Lady Middleton has her children in after dinner in *Sense and Sensibility*, as do the Coles in *Emma*: "The dessert succeeded, the children came in, and were talked to and admired."

Matters were more casual when the family dined alone or with close friends. The men might still linger over their wine, as Sir Thomas and Edmund do in *Mansfield Park* when discussing Fanny's future, but they seemed just as likely to join the women for an activity. In nice weather, walking was a favorite pastime. Although *Emma*'s Mr. Woodhouse always takes a little nap before tea, Emma and most of her acquaintances seem to prefer walking: "Emma and Harriet were going to walk; [Mr. Knightly] joined them; and, on returning, they fell in with a larger party . . . . They all united; and, on reaching Hartfield gates, Emma, who knew it was exactly the sort of visiting that would be welcome to her father, pressed them all to go in and drink tea with him."

A Quiet Family Evening

Evening teatime could be casual when just the family was present. A family such as the Austens would probably boil a copper kettle on the hob grate in the drawing room and use the second-best teapot and teacups to serve out the tea, which would be accompanied only by toast or slices of bread and butter. Wealthier families no doubt distinguished less between company teas and family teas. Such a family probably still had the full ceremony of servants carrying in the silver tea urn, bubbling and hissing, accompanied by elegant breads and cakes. Jane Austen described such a scene in *Mansfield Park*: "The solemn procession, headed by Baddeley [the butler], of tea-board, urn, and cake-bearers."

The women of the family made the tea. Men seem to have been considered quite incapable of making tea, no doubt because it was perilously close to cooking. In Jane Austen's time, servants almost never prepared the tea, either, because tea was too expensive to be entrusted to them. In an era when the family maid might be selling even used tea leaves out the back door, her employers certainly didn't want to trust her with new tea. The lady of the house generally made the tea herself, though she could deputize her daughters or another female family member. Lady Bertram, who can barely stay awake long enough to drink her tea, let alone make it, lets her sister, the officious Mrs. Norris, prepare the tea. When Mrs. Norris is unavailable, her niece Fanny makes it.

After tea was over, the family would often stay together in the drawing room, especially when short days and cold weather made being in a heated, well-lit room desirable. For less wealthy households, gathering in one room for the evening also had the added benefit of saving expensive fuel and candles. Families entertained themselves in various ways. Cards and other games were often played, even when there were no guests. The Austens, a creative family, sometimes amused themselves by composing and acting out charades and plays. Like many families, the Austens enjoyed reading aloud to one another.

Families differed in their opinions as to whether novels were appropriate reading material, or whether reading should be confined to "improving" books. In *Pride and Prejudice*, the Bennets offer Mr. Collins a novel to read aloud: "He started back, and begging pardon, protested that he never read novels. . . . Other books were produced, and after some deliberation he chose Fordyce's Sermons." The Austens, Jane said, were "great Novel-readers & not ashamed of being so." In her letters, Jane often mentioned the books the family was currently reading. "We have got the 2d vol. of Espriella's Letters, & I read it aloud by candlelight," she told Cassandra. Another time she wrote, "We changed [the book] for the 'Female Quixotte', which now makes our evening amusement; to me a very high one." When Cassandra was staying with their brother Edward and his wife, Elizabeth, Jane reported that "My father reads Cowper to us in the evening, to which I listen when I can. How do you spend your Evenings?—I guess that Eliz:th works, that you read to her, & that Edward goes to sleep."

Elizabeth's "work" was stitchery of some sort, a daily employment for most women of the time. The work might be useful, like Fanny Price's sewing for the poor in *Mansfield Park*, or decorative, like Lady Bertram's "long piece of needlework, of little use and no beauty." The education of young ladies was planned with an eye to their becoming "accomplished"; that is, learning both useful and elegant sewing skills, as well as having "a thorough knowledge of music, singing, drawing, dancing, and the modern languages," as Miss Bingley stipulates in *Pride and Prejudice*.

One of the reasons young ladies were expected to become musically "accomplished" is that they often provided

The evening was heavy like the day.—"I cannot think what is the matter with me!" said Lady Bertram, when the tea-things were removed. "I feel quite stupid. It must be sitting up so late last night. Fanny, you must do something to keep me awake. I cannot work. Fetch the cards,—I feel so very stupid." The cards were brought, and Fanny played at cribbage with her aunt till bed-time; and as Sir Thomas was reading to himself, no sounds were heard in the room for the next two hours beyond the reckonings of the game.

— *Mansfield Park*

the chief entertainment for an evening, whether at home or visiting. They might sing, or play an instrument such as the harp (as Mary Crawford does in *Mansfield Park*) or the pianoforte (as Jane Austen herself did). In *Emma*, both Miss Fairfax and Emma play the pianoforte for their friends' entertainment, pleasing Mr. Knightley greatly: "I do not know a more luxurious state, sir, than sitting at one's ease to be entertained a whole evening by two such young women; sometimes with music and sometimes with conversation."

A woman's talents, or "resources," as the annoying and presumptuous Mrs. Elton in *Emma* terms them, kept her and her family from boredom. "I always say a woman cannot have too many resources—and I feel very thankful that I have so many myself as to be quite independent of society," says Mrs. Elton, though she never stays home long enough for her resources to be tested: "From Monday next to Saturday, I assure you we have not a disengaged day!—A woman with fewer resources than I have, need not have been at a loss."

Pleasant Little Parties

Not all families were as creative as the Austens, and not all women had the "resources" of Mrs. Elton. For such families, visitors could enliven what would otherwise be a dull evening. In *Emma*, though Emma herself is a very talented young woman, she finds the prospect of spending long evenings alone with her father disheartening. Mr. Woodhouse is "a nervous man, easily depressed," who must be coddled and entertained to be kept happy. When there are no guests, Emma must hope "by the help of backgammon, to get her father tolerably through the evening." Fortunately, most evenings she is able to gather a few friends to join her father for tea and cards.

Visiting friends for tea could be an informal occasion, as when Jane wrote to Cassandra, "Sam Arnold dropt in to tea," or when she reported, "Last night, an accidental meeting & a sudden impulse produced Miss Benn & Maria Middleton at our Tea Table." In *Sense and Sensibility*, Colonel Brandon has a standing invitation to take tea and spend his evenings with Mrs. Jennings. Her sociable son-in-law, Sir John Middleton, appears constitutionally incapable of spending an evening with only his

> We drank tea again yesterday with the Tilsons, & met the Smiths.—I find all these little parties very pleasant.
>
> — Letter from Jane Austen to Cassandra, 18 April 1811

family around him. He often calls at the Dashwoods' cottage to insist, "You *must* drink tea with us tonight, for we shall be quite alone."

Casual visitors often participated in the family's normal evening activities. When Miss Benn visited the Austens once for dinner and tea, they included her in their reading aloud of *Pride and Prejudice*, which was newly arrived from the publisher. Miss Benn, a poor, middle-aged woman who is supposed by many to have been a model for Miss Bates in *Emma*, was unaware that Jane was the author. It pleased Jane to watch her reactions and report them to Cassandra: "She was amused, poor soul!"

Other teatime visits were more ceremonious, with invitations issued well ahead of the event and entertainments (often card games) planned for the guests. To amuse her father, Emma invites Mrs. Bates (who is "almost past every thing but tea and quadrille"), Miss Bates, and Mrs. Goddard, the local schoolmistress. Mrs. Goddard is a "plain, motherly kind of woman, who had worked hard in her youth, and now thought herself entitled to the occasional holiday of a tea-visit; and having formerly owed much to Mr. Woodhouse's kindness, felt his particular claim on her to leave her neat parlour, hung round with fancy-work whenever she could, and win or lose a few sixpences by his fireside."

On these more formal visits, the best china would be brought out and the best drawing room opened. In *The Watsons*, an unexpected friend visits the family at teatime, only to find important guests already there: "Instead of being shown into the usual little sitting room, the door of the best parlour a foot larger each way than the other was thrown open, & he beheld a circle of smart people whom he c[oul]d not immediately recognize arranged with all the honours of visiting round the fire, & Miss Watson sitting at the best Pembroke Table, with the best Tea things before her."

The Austen family often visited or were visited by friends for tea and cards. "Mrs Busby drinks tea & plays at Cribbage here tomorrow," Jane wrote to Cassandra, "& on friday I believe we go to the Chamberlaynes." The Austens, who were far from rich, seem to have fulfilled a good many of their social obligations with invitations to tea. Tea parties offered a less expensive way of entertaining friends than having them to dinner. Dinner parties at that time could mean two full courses, each consisting of many expensive dishes, not to mention wine and dessert. In contrast, refreshments served with tea were generally light—bread, toast, muffins, buns, or perhaps cake. "We ate 3 of the Buns [during the trip]," Jane reported once to Cassandra after arriving at her brother's house, "the remaining 3 made an elegant entertainment for Mr & Mrs Tilson who drank tea with us."

An evening of tea, conversation, cards, and quiet bun-nibbling, while not terribly exciting, could be a calm, pleasant way to pass the time. Jane Austen liked such "quiet tea-drinkings" with friends and family, but she wasn't thrilled when social duty forced her to mingle with people she found tedious or less than congenial. "A message came this afternoon from Mrs Latouche and Miss East, offering themselves to drink tea with us tomorrow," she wrote to Cassandra. "I am heartily sorry they are coming! It will be an Eveng spoilt to Fanny & me."

On the other hand, such dutiful entertaining did force Jane to socialize with people who no doubt inspired many of the ridiculous or unpleasant characters in her books. Outwardly polite and pleasant, she stored up her impressions of such people and passed them on to Cassandra: "Miss Milles was queer as usual & provided us with plenty to laugh at. She . . . talked on about it for half an hour, using such odd expressions & so foolishly minute that I could hardly keep my countenance."

Tea could also form a separate social event following a dinner party. In *Emma*, the Coles host such a party, and it is understood that their dinner guests will stay for tea and the rest of the evening's entertainments. Other guests, however, are invited to arrive only after the meal is over, to take tea and to spend the rest of the evening. Emma, the leader of society in Highbury, is naturally one of the dozen or so guests invited for the dinner itself. "The male part of Mr. Cox's family" are also among the chosen, but "the less worthy females were to come in the evening, with Miss Bates, Miss Fairfax, and Miss Smith." Perhaps the Coles' dining table could accommodate only so many, but the phrasing clearly conveys Jane Austen's opinion that being relegated to the after-dinner portion of the evening was a bit insulting. Insulting or not, it was a very common practice at the time, and Jane's slightly bitter tone may have come from her own experiences. As unmarried women closer in wealth and social status to Miss Bates than to Emma, she and Cassandra may often have been assigned to the after-dinner group.

An Elegant Entertainment

One step up from the quiet tea-and-cards evening was the evening party. Guests at such parties would expect other entertainments (such as performances by professional musicians) as well as tea and cards. After visiting the Maitland family one evening, Jane told Cassandra, "We found ourselves tricked into a thorough party at Mrs Maitlands, a quadrille & a Commerce Table, & Music in the other room." Such elegance didn't necessarily impress Jane: "The Miss M[aitland]s. were as civil & as silly as usual."

A dinner for a few select friends might precede the evening party, or it might not. In *Persuasion*, the insufferably arrogant Elizabeth Elliot knows

[Mrs. Elton] would soon shew them how every thing ought to be arranged. In the course of the spring she must return their civilities by one very superior party—in which her card tables should be set out with their separate candles and unbroken packs in the true style—and more waiters engaged for the evening than their own establishment could furnish, to carry round the refreshments at exactly the proper hour, and in the proper order.

— *Emma*

that her family's recently reduced financial circumstances will be revealed if she hosts a dinner party for the visiting Musgroves. She determines to hold an evening party only, which she justifies to herself on the grounds of elegance: "We do not profess to give dinners—few people in Bath do—Lady Alicia never does. . . . I will ask them all for an evening; that will be much better—that will be a novelty and a treat. . . . It shall be a regular party—small, but most elegant."

Tea was always served at evening parties, but the other refreshments were naturally of a superior nature compared with typical teatime fare, and took more planning than merely telling the cook to prepare some bread and butter. In *Emma*, Mrs. Elton had lived in Bath, which "made evening-parties perfectly natural to her." She is not impressed by the refreshments at the Highbury parties, being "shocked . . . at the poor attempt at rout-cakes, and there being no ice in the Highbury card parties." Rout cakes are little cookies (biscuits), and "ice" means ices or ice cream. A fashionable lady (such as Mrs. Elton imagines herself to be) knew that her reputation as a hostess depended on offering her guests properly prepared and expensive treats.

Jane Austen's brother Henry and his wife, Eliza (the fashionable former Countess de Feuillide), lived in London and were well acquainted with what guests expected at a truly elegant evening party. During one of Jane's visits, they held a musical party, with five professional musicians providing the entertainment. Eliza worked for days ahead of time to ensure its success. Jane sent Cassandra the details:

> Our party went off extremely well. There were many solicitudes, alarms & vexations beforehand of course, but at last everything was quite right. The rooms were dressed up with flowers &c, & looked very pretty. . . . Including everybody we were 66—which was considerably more than Eliza had expected, & quite enough to fill the Back Draw[in]g room, & leave a few to be scattered about in the other, & in the passage. . . . The House was not clear till after 12.

An evening party might end in an impromptu dance, as happened following the Coles' dinner party. In her letters, Jane often mentioned small dances or evening parties that ended in dancing. One had to be careful in London, though, where such informal rompings might be seen as provincial. In *Sense and Sensibility*, the Middletons, newly arrived in London, hold a small dance:

> Sir John had contrived to collect around him, nearly twenty young people, and to amuse them with a ball. This was an affair, however, of which Lady Middleton did not approve. In the country, an unpremeditated dance was very allowable; but in London, where the reputation of elegance was more important and less easily attained, it was risking too much for

the gratification of a few girls, to have it known that Lady Middleton had given a small dance of eight or nine couple, with two violins, and a mere side-board collation.

"*Every thing so good!*"

In Jane Austen's era, tea was invariably served at the more splendid evening entertainments, whether they were public affairs such as concerts or assemblies (public dances), or private balls. Ladies and gentlemen often went straight from their evening tea tables to the entertainment, yet once there they expected to be offered tea again. Tea was frequently included in the price of admission to a concert or assembly, but sometimes it was optional. After Jane attended one such assembly, she reported to Cassandra, "We paid an additional shilling for our Tea, which we took as we chose in an adjoining, & very comfortable room."

Obviously, tea was free of charge at private balls. At the Westons' ball in *Emma*, guests are offered tea and coffee as they arrive, which delights Miss Bates: "No coffee, I thank you, for me—never take coffee.—A little tea if you please, sir, by and bye,—no hurry—Oh! here it comes. Every thing so good!" The Westons choose to serve tea at the beginning of their ball, but hosts more typically offered tea during an intermission in the entertainment or dancing. Tea was generally set out in a separate room, to which everyone eagerly trooped at the break. Each gentleman escorted the lady with whom he had been dancing when tea was announced.

At public assemblies, each attending group of people seems to have had its own teapot, meaning assembly rooms needed to own a large stock of tea equipment. Indeed, for the New, or Upper, Assembly Rooms at Bath, records from the time show the purchase of hundreds of teapots and teacups. Gentlemen were in charge of procuring tea for the ladies in their party. In

Northanger Abbey, when Catherine Morland attends her first assembly at the Upper Rooms, she has no dancing partner to escort her to tea. She and Mrs. Allen squeeze themselves in at a table that is already occupied, only to find themselves tea-less. "Had not we better go away as it is?" asks Catherine. "Here are no tea things for us, you see." Eventually a gentleman at the table takes pity on them and helps them to tea.

Jane Austen often used the tea interval as a setting for humorous or emotionally fraught scenes in her novels. In *Persuasion*, Anne Elliot attends a concert at the Upper Rooms, where she hopes to see Captain Wentworth:

> The first act was over. Now she hoped for some beneficial change; and, after a period of nothing-saying amongst the party, some of them did decide on going in quest of tea. Anne was one of the few who did not choose to move. She remained in her seat, and . . . did not mean . . . to shrink from conversation with Captain Wentworth, if he gave her the opportunity. . . . He did not come however. Anne sometimes fancied she discerned him at a distance, but he never came. The anxious interval wore away unproductively.

Everybody was shortly in motion for tea, and they must squeeze out like the rest. . . . When at last arrived in the tea-room, she felt yet more the awkwardness of having no party to join, no acquaintance to claim, no gentleman to assist them. They . . . were obliged to sit down at the end of a table, at which a large party were already placed, without having anything to do there, or anybody to speak to, except each other.

— *Northanger Abbey*

After tea, the dancing or other entertainment resumed. In *The Watsons*, Jane Austen describes the crush that often ensued when tea was over: "On rising from Tea, there was again a scramble for the pleasure of being first out of the room, which happened to be increased by one or two of the card parties having just broken up, & the players being disposed to move exactly the different way."

As long as she was in the company of friends, Jane Austen seems to have enjoyed going to balls and assemblies, unlike some of the smaller parties where her sense of courtesy compelled her to be pleasant to people she didn't care for. "I hate tiny parties" she told Cassandra, "they force one into constant exertion." But even while enjoying herself, she was ever on the watch for amusing characters. Having spotted a woman at an assembly in Bath who was said to be an adulteress, she reported to Cassandra, "She was highly rouged, & looked rather quietly & contentedly silly than anything else."

A Splendid Supper

Whether the entertainment consisted of quiet conversation, an elegant party, an impromptu dance, or a formal ball, private evening entertainments sometimes included supper, and supper often included tea. Jane once wrote to Cassandra describing the evening party their teenaged niece had attended: "Anna . . . had a delightful Evening with the Miss Middletons— Syllabub, Tea, Coffee, Singing, Dancing, a Hot Supper, eleven o'clock, everything that can be imagined agreable."

By Jane Austen's time, hot suppers such as her niece had enjoyed were becoming less common. In Jane's youth, the early dinner times left people hungry by the middle of the evening; understandably, they favored large, sit-down suppers. As dinner times drifted later, following one full meal with another only three hours or so afterward seemed unnecessary. Suppers moved from the formal, cloth-covered table to the sideboard, where people generally served themselves. The new style of informal supper ranged from a few tidbits or sandwiches and wine set out on a tray for the family, to elegant repasts suitable for a party. A novel of the period, *Vicissitudes in Genteel Life*, describes a party supper:

> The evening of this happy day was concluded in dancing;
> card-playing &c. We had not any formal supper, but in one of
> the apartments were some side-boards; with several tables for
> tea; coffee &c. Wine; negus; rich cakes of divers kinds;
> sweetmeats, foreign and English; wet and dry; creams; jellies
> and fruit; with one board of cold chicken; potted meats, &c.
> &c. completed the viands.

In *Emma*, Mr. Woodhouse (never a man to take up modern practices) loves to serve sit-down suppers to his guests "because it had been the fashion of his youth." Supper dishes at the Woodhouses' home include baked apples, biscuits, "a delicate fricassee of sweetbread and some asparagus," boiled eggs, minced chicken, scalloped oysters, and apple tarts, though the guests don't always get the chance to eat the food. Mr. Woodhouse, who limits himself to gruel for supper and who assumes everyone's digestion must be as delicate as his own, often disappoints his guests by sending dishes away because he fears the rich foods will harm their health.

Dishes for a Grand Entertainment

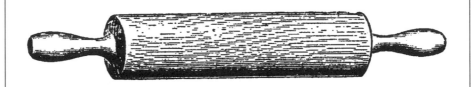

Small Rout Cakes

Rub into one pound of dried and sifted flour, half a pound of butter, six ounces of pounded and sifted loaf sugar, and the yolks of two well-beaten eggs; mix them all into a paste with a little rose water; divide the quantity, put a few dried currants or caraway seeds into one half; roll out the paste, cut it into small round cakes, and bake them upon buttered tins.

— from *The Practice of Cookery*, 1840

In Jane Austen's day, a "rout" was a fashionable evening party. Rout cakes are a kind of little shortbread cookie (biscuit) that often contain dried fruit. This recipe produces two types, making a nice variety for your own elegant routs. If you wish to be completely authentic, you can sometimes find rose water at shops that specialize in Middle Eastern or Asian foods; be sure the kind you purchase is edible, as there are many scented rose oil mixtures on the market meant just for potpourri. Pure vanilla extract makes a satisfactory substitute.

Rout Cakes for Mrs. Elton

8 oz/ 225 g/ 1 cup butter, room temperature
6 oz/ 170 g/ 3/4 cup + 2 tablespoons white sugar
2 egg yolks, well beaten
2 teaspoons rose water or pure vanilla extract
1 pound/ 450 g/ 3-3/4 cups sifted white flour
3 oz/ 85 g/ 1/2 cup dried currants
1 teaspoon caraway seeds

Preheat oven to 350° F/ 180° C/ Gas Mark 4.

Cream the butter and the sugar together. Stir in the egg yolks and rose water or vanilla. Mix until well blended. Stir in the flour gradually. Divide the dough into two parts. Fold the currants into one half and the caraway seeds into the other half. Roll out about 1/4 inch (6 mil) thick, and cut out into small rounds. Bake on a greased baking sheet 15–20 minutes or until the edges just begin to turn golden. Makes 24 small cookies.

The hedge-hog, the hen and chickens in jelly, the Solomon's temple, and the eggs and bacon, &c. in flummery . . . may, with propriety, be classed among the elegant ornaments for a grand entertainment.

— *The London Art of Cookery*, 1807

Solid Syllabubs

Put in a pint of white wine to a quart of rich cream, the juice of four lemons, and sugar it to your taste. Whip it up well, take off the froth as it rises, and put it upon a hair sieve. Let it stand till the next day in a cool place, then fill your glasses better than half full with the thin, put on the froth, and heap it as high as you can. It will keep for several days, and the bottom look clear.

— *The London Art of Cookery*, 1807

These syllabubs, fun and very easy to make, are a splendid-looking addition to your grand entertainment. The froth looks like whipped cream but stacks up like a soft meringue. An electric mixer is so efficient that there is no "thin" left over after the cream whips up, so if you want to serve them in the old manner, you'll have to use extra wine or lemonade to fill your glasses first. Syllabubs may be made a day ahead.

Solid Syllabubs

8 fl oz/ 225 ml/ 1 cup white wine or lemonade
16 fl oz/ 1/2 litre/ 2 cups heavy cream
Juice of two lemons (4 tablespoons)
2 tablespoons powdered (icing) sugar

Stir all the ingredients together, then whip the mixture with an electric mixer on medium-high speed (or with a wire whisk if you have the strength and the time). Whip until the mixture forms soft peaks (about 5 minutes). Scoop the froth into a fine-mesh strainer placed atop a large bowl to drain for a few minutes (there will be very little liquid to drain out). Spoon into individual dessert dishes or on top of wine or lemonade in glasses filled "better than half full." Refrigerate until serving time. Makes eight 3/4-cup servings.

Though we eat little flesh and drink no wine,
Yet let's be merry: we'll have tea and toast;
Custards for supper, and an endless host
Of syllabubs and jellies and mince-pies,
And other such lady-like luxuries,—
Feasting on which we will philosophize!

— "Letter to Maria Gisborne" by Percy Bysshe Shelley, 1820

THE REGENT.

The Regent's, or George the Fourth's, Punch

Pare as thin as possible the rinds of two China oranges, of two lemons, and of one Seville orange, and infuse them for an hour in half a pint of thin cold syrup; then add to them the juice of the fruit. Make a pint of strong green tea, sweeten it well with fine sugar, and when it is quite cold, add it to the fruit and syrup, with a glass of the best old Jamaica rum, a glass of brandy, one of arrack, one of pine-apple syrup, and two bottles of champagne; pass the whole through a fine lawn sieve until it is perfectly clear, then bottle and put it into ice until dinner is served. We are indebted for this receipt to a person who made the punch daily for the prince's table, at Carlton palace, for six months; it has been in our possession some years, and may be relied on.

— *Modern Cookery for Private Families*, 1845

The Prince Regent, a man of large appetites in so many ways, apparently liked his punch strong. When he overindulged, as he commonly did, the tea in it may have been the only thing that kept him vertical. The recipe below is based on simpler versions from the time, and is a wonderful punch for celebrations and balls.

Regent's Punch for the Westons' Ball

4 large lemons (organic, if using the peel)
16 fl oz/ 1/2 litre/ 2 cups water
3 teaspoons of loose green tea (or the contents of 3 teabags)
8 oz/ 225 g/ 1-1/2 cups powdered (icing) sugar
1 bottle of chilled champagne or sparkling wine (or clear soda pop, if
  preferred)

Roll the lemons on a table to make them juicier. Pare the zest (only the
yellow part of the rind) of the lemons. Cut the remaining white rind from
the pulp, remove the seeds, then chop the pulp coarsely. Discard the white
rind and the seeds. In a nonreactive pan, boil the water, pulp, and zest for 10
minutes. Let the mixture cool for 1 minute, then pour it over the tea leaves
in a heat-proof bowl or teapot. Stir, then let steep 3 minutes. Strain through
a fine mesh strainer. Stir in the sugar and chill. To serve, pour the chilled
mixture into a punch bowl or pitcher, then stir in the chilled champagne.

An even easier version: Make a pint (1/2 litre) of strong green tea,
strain, and chill. In a punch bowl, mix the chilled tea and a 12-ounce (355
ml) can of frozen lemonade concentrate. Add sugar to taste. Pour in a bottle
of chilled champagne, and serve.

"A good dish of Tea"
Making the Perfect Cup

As in all cooking, success in making tea lies in the quality of the ingredients used. Tea leaves of inferior quality and unpleasant-tasting water will not provide a wonderful tea experience, to say the least. Always use freshly drawn water. Water that is boiled more than once has less oxygen, reducing the flavor and aroma of your tea.

Most supermarket tea bags contain a decent quality of leaves and produce an acceptable cup of tea, but tea experts say that for a really good cup you need loose tea. The leaves of loose tea are generally larger than those in teabags, and the tea itself is often of a higher quality. Many tea companies make delightful blends, and it's fun to experiment with different kinds until you find the ones that suit you best. Store your tea in airtight containers, as it easily picks up odors.

The amount of tea to use per cup has been the subject of great debate, but most authorities suggest one teaspoonful of leaves for each cup of water. Some teas are lighter in character, and you may need to try different quantities until you find just the right amount for your taste.

Tea steeps best when it is kept warm during the process. Some people claim

"What in the name of common sense is to recommend Brinshore? A most insalubrious air—roads proverbially detestable—water Brackish beyond example, impossible to get a good dish of Tea within 3 miles of the place."

— Mr. Parker in *Sanditon*

earthenware teapots are better than china ones, on the grounds that they retain heat better. Whichever type of teapot you choose, warm it by rinsing it with boiling water right before you make the tea. Using a tea cozy also helps keep in the heat during steeping.

Some tea lovers prefer to let the tea leaves float freely in the teapot, but using a tea ball permits you to remove the leaves to prevent over-steeping. Use the largest tea ball you can find, and fill it only half full so the tea leaves have room to expand.

For dark oolong, black, and herbal teas, use water that is at a full boil (212°F/100°C) as it hits the tea leaves. How long you steep it is a matter of personal preference, but five minutes for most black teas and herbal teas and seven minutes for dark oolongs usually give very nice results.

Light oolong, white, and green teas are made with cooler water, about 180°F/82°C. Judging when the water has reached this temperature can prove difficult, but when your tea kettle begins to make a rumbling noise is often about right. White tea should be steeped about seven minutes, but light oolongs and green teas for only about three minutes to avoid bitterness.

Regardless of the type of tea, remove the leaves from the teapot when the tea is done steeping. If you leave them in, the tea will over-steep and taste bitter.

Homemade iced tea is easy to prepare and tasty to drink. Just make the tea with double the amount of tea leaves you would ordinarily use. When the tea is ready, pour it into ice-filled glasses, sweeten to your taste, and garnish the glasses with slices of lemon.

Hot tea supposedly tastes the same whether served in a simple stoneware mug or in the finest of china, but let's be honest: drinking your tea out of a beautifully flowered china cup makes the experience a special one. Get out your best teapot, and the prettiest cup and saucer you own. Sit down with your favorite Jane Austen book and enjoy.

Bibliography

Jane Austen: Her Works and Her Times

Acton, Eliza, *Modern Cookery for Private Families*, 1845, reprinted 2002.

Austen, Caroline, *My Aunt Jane Austen* (1867). Printed for the Jane Austen Society, 1952, new ed., 1991.

Austen, James and Henry, *The Loiterer*, No. I, January 31, 1789, No. IV, February 21, 1789.*

Austen, Jane, *Sense and Sensibility* (1811).

_____, *Pride and Prejudice* (1813).

_____, *Mansfield Park* (1814).

_____, *Emma* (1816).

_____, *Northanger Abbey* (1818).

_____, *Persuasion* (1818).

_____, *The Works of Jane Austen*, vi, Minor Works, ed. R.W. Chapman, Oxford, 1954.

_____, *Jane Austen's Letters*, ed. Deirdre Le Faye, Oxford, 3rd ed., 1995.

Austen-Leigh, James-Edward, *A Memoir of Jane Austen*, 2nd ed., London, 1871.*

Austen-Leigh, William and Richard, rev. and enlarged by Deirdre Le Faye, *Jane Austen: A Family Record*, London, 1989.

Brabourne, Edward, 1st Lord. *Letters of Jane Austen*, London, 1884.*

Burney, Fanny, *The Journals and Letters of Fanny Burney.*

Burnett, T.A.J., *The Rise & Fall of a Regency Dandy*, Great Britain, 1981.

Corley, T.A.B., "Jane Austen's 'real, honest, old-fashioned Boarding-school': Mrs La Tournelle and Mrs Goddard," in *Women's Writing*, Vol. 5, No. 1, 1998.*

Farley, John, *The London Art of Cookery*, 11th ed., London, 1807, reprinted 1988.

"Farther Observations on the Ill Effects of this Liquor by a learned Physician," in *Gentleman's Magazine* Vol. 7 Apr 1737. pp. 214-215.*

Girouard, Mark, *Life in the English Country House*, London, 1978.

Glasse, Hannah, *The Art of Cookery Made Plain and Easy*, London 1796, facsimile 1971.

Haythornthwaite, Philip J., *The Armies of Wellington*, London, 1994.

Hesketh, Christian, et al., *The Country House Cookery Book*, New York, 1985.

Hill, Constance, *Jane Austen, Her Homes and Her Friends*, London, 1901.*

Honan, Park, *Jane Austen: Her Life*, New York, 1989.

Irving, Washington, *Sketchbook*, 1819.*

Johnson, Samuel, "Review of A Journal of Eight Days' Journey," originally published in *Literary Magazine 2*, no. 13, 1757.*

Kincaid, Captain John, *Adventures in the Rifle Brigade*, 1830, reprinted 1997.

Lane, Maggie, *A Charming Place: Bath in the Life and Novels of Jane Austen*, Bath, 1988, reprinted 2000.

_____, *Jane Austen and Food*, London, 1995.

Le Faye, Deirdre, *Jane Austen, The World of Her Novels*, New York, 2002.

_____, *Jane Austen's 'Outlandish Cousin': The Life and Letters of Eliza de Feuillide*, London, 2002.

Lejeune, Baron Louis-François, Memoirs of Baron Lejeune, trans. Mrs. Arthur Bell (N. D'Anvers), London, 1897.*

Leslie, Eliza, *Seventy-Five Receipts for Pastry, Cakes, and Sweetmeats*, Boston, 1828, reprinted 1989.

The Mirror of Graces, by a Lady of Distinction, London, 1811, facsimile 1997.

Mitford, Mary Russell, *Our Village*, first published in the *Lady's Magazine*, 1819, 1893 ed.*

Nicolson, Nigel, *The World of Jane Austen*, London, 1991.

O'Brian, Patrick, *Men-of-War: Life in Nelson's Navy*, New York, 1995.

"Observations on the Effects of Tea," in *Gentleman's Magazine* Vol. 7 Apr 1737, pp. 213-214.*

Picard, Liza, *Dr. Johnson's London*, New York, 2001.

Pope, Dudley, *Life in Nelson's Navy*, Annapolis, Maryland, 1981.

"The Proceedings of the Old Bailey London 1674 to 1834" (tea-smuggling cases), available online at http://www.oldbaileyonline.org/

Rogers, H.A., *Views of Some of the Most Celebrated By-Gone Pleasure Gardens of London, with Some Contemporary Descriptions thereof (Chiefly Poetical), Collection from Various Sources*, London, 1896.*

Shelley, Henry C., *Inns and Taverns of Old London*, Boston, 1909*

Smith, Sir Harry, *The Autobiography of Lt. General Sir Harry Smith*, London, 1902.*

Southam, Brian, *Jane Austen and the Navy*, London, 2000.

Taylor, Joseph, *Nature the best Physician; or, a Complete Domestic Herbal*, London, 1818, quoted in Brown, Alice Cooke, *Early American Herb Recipes*, New York, 1966.

Tomalin, Claire, *Jane Austen: A Life*, New York, 1998.

Vickery, Amanda, *The Gentleman's Daughter*, Great Britain, 1998.

White, Joshua , *Letters from England*, 1810.*

Wildeblood, Joan and Peter Brinson, *The Polite World: A Guide to English Manners and Deportment from the Thirteenth to the Nineteenth Century*. London, 1965.

Woodford, Rev. James, *The Diary of a Country Parson 1758-1802*, ed. John Beresford, London, 1949.

Books about Tea

Chow, Kit and Ione Kramer, *All the Tea in China*, San Francisco, 1990.

Faulknew, Rupert, ed., *Tea East & West*, London, 2003.

Francis Leggett & Co., *Tea Leaves*, 1900.*

Gray, Arthur, *The Little Tea Book*, New York, 1903.

Okakura, Kakuzo, *The Book of Tea*, New York, 1906.*

Pettigrew, Jane, *A Social History of Tea*, London, 2001.

Pratt, James Norwood, *New Tea Lover's Treasury*, San Francisco, California, 1999.

Repplier, Agnes, *To Think of Tea!*, Cambridge, Massachusetts, 1932.

Schivelbusch, Wolfgang, *Tastes of Paradise: A Social History of Spices, Stimulants, and Intoxicants*, New York, 1992.

Twining, Sam, *My Cup of Tea*, London, 2002.

Ukers, William H., *All About Tea*, New York, 1935.

_____, *The Romance of Tea: An Outline History of Tea and Tea-Drinking through Sixteen Hundred Years*, New York and London, 1936.

Weinberg, Bennett Alan and Bonnie K. Bealer, *The World of Caffeine: The Science and Culture of the World's Most Popular Drug*, New York, 2002.

Period Novels and Poetry

Anne of Swansea, *Lovers and Friends; or, Modern Attachments*, London, 1821. CH

Bennett, Anna Maria, *Agnes De-Courci: A Domestic Tale*, London, 1789. CH

Brady, Dr. Nicholas (1659-1726), "The Tea Table," quoted in Ukers, *Romance of Tea*.

Burney, Frances, *Camilla; or, A Picture of Youth*, London, 1796.*

Caroline; or, the Diversities of Fortune, London, 1787. CH

Cowper, William, "The Task: The Winter Evening," (1785) in *Poems*, vol. II, New York, 1814.

Edgeworth, Maria, *The Absentee*, 1812.*

_____, *Moral Tales for Young People*, 1805.*

_____, *The Parent's Assistant*, 1796.*

_____, *Patronage*, 1813.*

_____, *Popular Tales*, 1804.*

Jacson, Frances, *Isabella*, London, 1823. CH

Marryat, Captain Frederick, *The King's Own*, 1830.*

_____, *Mr. Midshipman Easy*, 1836.*

Matthews, Mrs., *Simple Facts; or, The History of an Orphan*, London, 1793. CH

Shelley, Percy Bysshe, "Letter to Maria Gisborne" (1820), from *Posthumous Poems* (1824)*

Smart, Christopher (1722-1771), "The Tea-Pot and Scrubbing Brush, A Fable"*

Smollett, Tobias, *Humphrey Clinker*, 1771, Modern Library ed., New York, 1929.

Vicissitudes in Genteel Life, Stafford, 1794. CH

Waller, Edmund (1606-1687), "Of Tea."*

Woty, William, "White Conduit House," 1760, quoted in Rogers.

* Online (electronic) edition used. Some texts are difficult to find in print, but are available online. The Project Gutenberg website http://www.gutenberg.net/ is one very good source for out-of-copyright texts.

CH Period novel available online at http://www.chawton.org/ from the Chawton House Library & Study Centre.

Index

For characters and places in Jane Austen's works, the names of the works in which they appear are abbreviated in parentheses: *Emma (E)*, *Mansfield Park (MP)*, *Minor Works (MW)*, *Northanger Abbey (NA)*, *Persuasion (P)*, *Pride and Prejudice (P&P)*, *Sanditon (S)*, *Sense and Sensibility (S&S)*, *The Watsons (TW)*